CAMPS AND CLIMBS
IN
ARCTIC NORWAY

Descent from the Trolltind (*Chapter IV*)

Camps and Climbs in Arctic Norway

by THOMAS WEIR

with 58 photographs by the author

CASSELL AND COMPANY LTD
LONDON

CASSELL & CO. LTD

37/38 St. Andrew's Hill, Queen Victoria Street
London, E.C.4

and at

210 Queen Street, Melbourne
26/30 Clarence Street, Sydney
Haddon Hall, City Road, Auckland, N.Z.
1068 Broadview Avenue, Toronto
122 East 55th Street, New York 22
Avenida 9 de Julho 1138, São Paulo
Galeria Güemes, Escritorio 518/520 Florida 165, Buenos Aires
Haroon Chambers, South Napier Road, Karachi
15 Graham Road, Ballard Estate, Bombay 1
17 Central Avenue P.O. Dharamtala, Calcutta
P.O. Box 275, Cape Town
P.O. Box 1386, Salisbury, S. Rhodesia
P.O. Box 959, Accra, Gold Coast
Calçada Do Carma 55–2º, Lisbon
25 rue Henri Barbusse, Paris 5e
Islands Brygge 5, Copenhagen

Set in 12 pt. Walbaum type and
printed in Great Britain by Butler & Tanner Ltd., Frome and London
F.353

CONTENTS

ILLUSTRATIONS

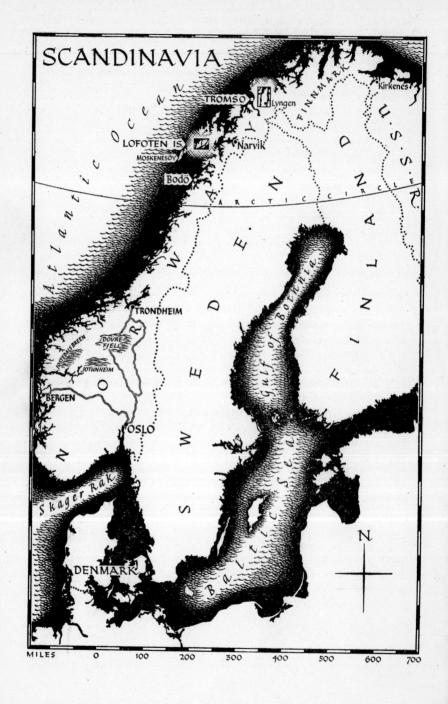

SCANDINAVIA

CHAPTER I

The Road North

WHEN the urge to go to out-of-the-way parts of the world is allied to lack of cash, economic geography becomes a fit subject of investigation. Such knowledge pays dividends, whether it is of the movements of Milk-Marketing-board lorries offering possibilities of lifts to remote glens of the Scottish Highlands, or of fishing boats plying between Grimsby and the Arctic Circle.

Our particular interest was in fishing boats; White Sea trawlers in fact. And our hopes of a passage were high, for one of our number, Adam Watson, was in touch with a man who had a friend, who knew a man aboard such a boat. Three of us were involved; Douglas Scott, Adam Watson, and myself, and briefly the plan was this: to climb and camp north of the Arctic Circle. We had fifty pounds apiece, and our intention was to stay up there just as long as that money lasted.

Tentatively we thought of beginning on the Lofotens, a group of islands which rise from the Arctic Ocean in fantastic rock spires. The Cuillin of Skye were nothing, we were told, compared to these peaks of fairy-like beauty springing straight out of the sea to jagged summits, some of which had never been climbed. Moreover, the low light of the midnight sun was said to infuse these peaks with colours richer than any Alpen glow, changing from gold to bronze, and copper, as one day gave way to the next.

1

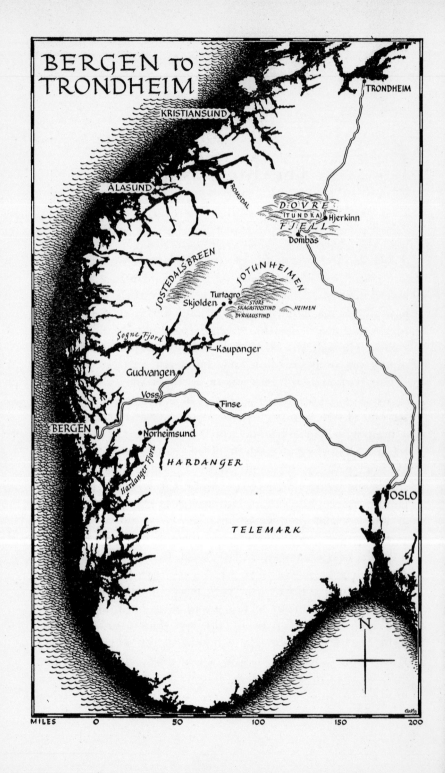

After Lofoten, some kind of transport being forthcoming, we planned to go to the peninsula of Lyngen, a lonely headland north of Tromso which contains the highest mountain in Arctic Norway, Jaeggevarre, the " Mont Blanc of the North ", where, according to Slingsby, " nature has developed her wildest and most eerie forms ".

Despite the indefinite line of communications to the White Sea trawler, we had every confidence in Adam. Two years before, this youth had done a return trip from Aberdeen to Iceland on a fishing boat, exploring much wild mountain country on a diet consisting largely of wild ducks' eggs. And while Scott and I had been in India with the Scottish Himalayan Expedition, he had travelled alone in Swedish Lapland and Finnmark, visiting the Russian border at Kirkenes, before heading south to Svolvær, capital of Lofoten. This time he had lived on fish, much of it caught by himself, a diet which, he said, was fresher than many of the eggs he had eaten.

The finish of this trip was an epic journey on two trawlers. One took him to the Faeroes, in seas so rough that all the crew were sick. Adam, meantime, lay in the fo'c'sle in a space like a rabbit hutch while the gale blew itself out and a fog rolled up, forcing them to lie tossing on the waves for yet another day. At each pitch of the vessel he got a new angle on his legs. Sometimes they were above him as if he was standing on his head, at other times below him as if he was standing up.

Ashore at Klakksvik he felt his luck was in when an Aberdeen trawler limped in for repairs. Episode Two, the crawl back to the granite city aboard this boat, began at half speed, but it became interesting when the ship's log broke down, and everyone was called upon to look out for the sight of land. Adam said he felt like Vasco da Gama.

Having heard this story in all its detail of sea-sickness, I was not particularly disappointed when he broached a new plan cutting out the trawler. If we cared to go to Bergen, Watson senior would be delighted to fall in with our wishes and motor us as far north as the road would take him. As this chance to see the interior of Norway was not to be missed, we jumped at it.

So, instead of taking a battering aboard a trawler, we sailed into Bergen aboard the luxury ship *Venus*, having parted with one fifth of our total cash on the one-way trip. Arriving in Bergen in the sunshine of July and finding half the population carrying umbrellas leads one to imagine the Norwegians to be a nation of pessimists. Once you know better, as we were to know within twenty-four hours, you call them realists, for it rains more in Bergen than in Manchester or Glasgow, and that means that it is very seldom dry.

We were lucky to hit a sunny day in Bergen, and so get an impression of steep green hills dotted with the bright yellow, white, and red squares of houses perched above the blue fjord, where the tall masts and funnels of Atlantic liners jostled with the orange and copper of packed fishing smacks. The old part of Bergen, with its deep alley-ways between wooden walls, particularly intrigued us.

All that we required of the town were a few necessary provisions. Not until we were in camp by a little lake, with the larder stocked, and the road stretching northward ahead of us, did we feel our holiday had begun.

Umbrellas were the order of the villages we passed through as we wormed in and out over the Hardanger Fjord, rain beating on the windscreen, and great waterfalls spouting over black crags. The route zig-zagged into fierce gorges of Himalayan depth, with forested slopes stretching upward to disappear in the swirl of mist, where rock pin-nacles sometimes thrust sensational fingers. We spiralled upward to arrive on the crest of a ridge. Below us the valley dropped two thousand feet in a steep wall.

Waterfalls we had thought large were tiny compared to those hemming this valley. We dropped in a series of " Devil's Elbows " alongside the most spectacular, a milk-white column of water spouting sheer for five hundred feet before bursting like a bomb in a gigantic convulsion of foam. This tower of spray fell a further two hundred feet before its final burst filled the air with fine drizzle.

Hairpin after hairpin saw us down to the floor of a narrow glen, gloomy as Glencoe. It terminated on the sea narrows of a fjord at a place called Gudvangen where a ferry awaited. The three-hour crossing was monotonous in the extreme, for the scene hardly changed. We were in the upper reaches of the longest fjord in Norway, the Sogne Fjord, but that misty day of rain hardly did credit to its dripping woods and dark water.

Things took a turn for the better on the other side. Suddenly the sun came out. The trees became a living green and the water sparkled. We put the tent up on the stubble of a hayfield by the edge of emerald water with whinchats and spotted fly-catchers for company. Flowers were thick as in an English lane, even to white and yellow stone-crop growing from the rocks.

For the first time we were able to go for a walk and shake off that feeling of frustration inseparable from imprisonment on four wheels. That still evening on the wooded shores of the Sogne Fjord had a quality of enchantment.

Strolling back to camp at 11 p.m., we heard the sound of an accordion and we followed it to its source, to a little clearing in the forest where a dancing platform had been erected. Gaily clad girls jigged up and down to the strains of the latest American dance tunes. The local lads stood around in shirt-sleeves, not yet having plucked up courage enough to ask for a dance. The sudden appearance of three trolls stopped the music.

The morning was delightful ; warm and still. The route lay over forested hills, above valleys straddled with the power lines of hydro-electricity. They were not an eyesore. They fitted the country as unobtrusively as railway lines, serving the nests of houses that cropped up in such unexpected places. I look forward to the day when the Scottish Highlands will have this sense of being " lived in ", instead of an artificial desolation of space.

By mid-day we had reached Skjolden and were soon mounting rapidly on the highest climbing road in Norway, clearing great wooded bluffs to enter a wild moorland terrain. Suddenly, round a bend and before us was a towering fang of glittering crag, Store Skagastolstind, the " Matterhorn of Norway ". All too well I could appreciate how Slingsby must have felt when he saw this unclimbed monster, and determined to reach its top.

Yet his delight was not so much in its mere conquest, but in the discovery that here was the best mountain yet. " Best " to him meant the mountain giving the finest sport, the hardest struggle, the greatest joy in the quest ; for in his mountaineering he bubbled over with an exuberant enthusiasm that made a high adventure of every climb.

He was not a mere record maker, or breaker. No other foreigner is likely to enjoy the veneration accorded to this great British mountaineer, a man who loved Norway and the Norwegians, who spoke their language, and took the trouble to read deeply into their ancient history, so that he could understand them more. His friendly ways and homely habits are legend to this day, and the high esteem in which British mountaineers are held in Norway today is largely due to him.

Unfortunately there was little chance of us climbing the Store. What had been falling as rain in the last few days had been snow on the high tops, hence the icy glitter of the peak. But its neighbour, the Dyrhaustind, was a different proposition. This looked an easy mountain, no more than four or five thousand feet above us, offering the prospect of wide views. We lost no time in pitching the tent and setting forth, climbing up to a frozen lake at the foot of the glacier coming down from between the two peaks.

From here we cut straight up the mountain-side, enjoying a rock scramble to the snow ridge of our peak. Before us was the country that had so fascinated Slingsby in the heyday of its exploration.

We looked on a lonely country ; from the plastic glisten of the far distant Jostedals Breen, 300 square miles of ice curling over sombre mountain walls in the largest ice sheet in Europe, to spikes of uncompromising gabbro that sprang up on three sides of us. This was the Jotunheim, home of the demons or frost giants, otherwise known as Jotuns. Guarded by yawning crevasses, bulging ice-falls and wrinkled glaciers, with the swirl of racing cloud breaking round their grim crests, it was easy to understand how they came to be so named. The feeling of mystery, of space, and of incredible wildness, aroused feelings in me experienced hitherto only in Scotland, where there is the same primal sweep of the untamed.

The snow ridge we had been following suddenly narrowed to a rock edge plastered in new snow. Rock pinnacles rose weirdly, shadows in space. We put on the rope and climbed an airy crest, climbing carefully on slippery holds. It was not difficult, but a slip on the part of an unroped man would have been fatal. The summit was a pinnacle barely big enough for four men. Unfortunately a dense screen of mist still hung on top, but lower down we came out of the cloud into sunshine, in time to see the surge of mist streamers fold and unfold round the gold-laced shoulders of the great Skagastolstind.

Having got up so easily we took the descent too lightly, glissading merrily, to be cut off by steep crags. Not without difficulty we got down to the tent at 9.30 p.m., the peak having taken only seven hours.

Unfortunately this good weather was short lived. The next day we were back to mist and rain—foul conditions for the crossing of the highest point in the road at 1,400 metres, a height greater than the summit of Ben Nevis. The scene up here was Arctic, ice floes drifting in steely lakes, snow banks clinging to roadside verges, and glacier snouts rising to mist-enshrouded peaks. The only birds were snow-buntings, their plumage matching perfectly this austerity landscape of soot and whitewash.

Down out of the mist to contour a lake and we sped through leagues of woodland to climb into a new kind of country, a country of birch scrub and bleak moorland, featureless except for a hamlet called Hjerkinn. We camped there at three thousand feet, and that night the first mosquitoes zoomed around the tent. The bumps they raised on hands and foreheads were a mere foretaste of what was to come later from these bloodthirsty rangers. Indeed, flies were the bane of Nordland camping, from common midges to large horse-flies that bit with the cunning of Highland clegs. Only the mosquito, however, is equipped with a snout long enough to bite through the thickness of woollen pullovers and socks.

The mist had cleared away by morning, and we saw around us rolling hills reminiscent of home, except that these hills were grey with reindeer moss and wreathed with great snow beds. This was the land of the famed tundra, of lakes and conifer woods, of large stretches of birch scrub ; the story-book country of reindeer and strange species of wild birds. Eagerly we set off on a little tour.

First thing to cross our path was a mealy redpoll, a bird seen occasionally in Britain in exceptionally hard winters. Here it was in its summer haunts, like its neighbours, the grey-headed wagtail and Lapland bunting. Colonies of fieldfares scattered from the trees at our approach, sociable birds even in summer. I had not expected to find them nesting in colonies. Brambling and redwing, golden plover and bobbing wheatears, were a few of the other birds we were delighted to see.

But the best find of all fell to Watson senior ; a snowy owl that flew out in his path, giving him a superb view of great ermine wings and plump sailing flight. Although we searched the forest hoping to flush it, we were unlucky. If only we had been able to spend more time we might have seen the common crane, blue throat, and dotterel.

1. Climbing through great wooded bluffs from Skjolden on the highest road in Norway. Moorland terrain and ice-peaks burst on the traveller in the next thousand feet (*Chapter I*)

2. First sight of the Store Skagastolstind, 7,874 feet high, the eighth highest mountain in Norway, situated in the range of the Horungtinder. The highest climbing road in Norway crosses the flank of this range, a road contouring icy lakes and winding its way through glaciers (*Chapter I*)

3. Trondheim, third city of Norway, situated on the estuary of the Nid. Every day a boat leaves this Northern town for the Arctic. Note the submarine pens (centre) built by the Germans in the late war (*Chapter I*)

4. Camp at 3,000 feet in the Dovre Fjell, showing the well-wooded slopes where a snowy owl was seen, and the hill-tops grey with reindeer moss (*Chapter I*)

5. This church of Svolvær is a landmark visible for miles out at sea. Behind the right-hand houses rises the island of Store Molla. Note (*left*) the incredible steepness of the peaks behind the town (*Chapter II*)

6. One of the many little inlets which makes Svolvæer such a delightful place. Beyond the fish-curing factory on the right is the island of Store Molla (*Chapter II*)

7: A corner of Svolvær harbour. The "horns" of the Svolvær "Goat" are on the right of centre ; a weird pinnacle so named by reason of the twin figures of rock crowning the great crag which rises sheer over the town (*Chapter II*)

8. Our trio. From left to right : Douglas Scott ; the Author ; Adam Watson. In homage to the first burst of sunshine we had experienced in the Lofotens, we donned shorts, but mosquitoes quickly drove us back into long trousers again (*Chapter II*)

9. The Svolvær "Goat". The route described lay straight up the middle of the face, between the right shoulder and the main wall. Then out across the niche to the Svolvær face sheer above the town. The topmost pinnacle was climbed by its right-hand edge. The lower pinnacle was attained by an airy jump through space
(Chapter II)

10. Having climbed the " Goat ", the best way down the difficult upper slab was to fix a double rope and slide down to the saddle sixty feet below. Scott relieves the strain on his arms by passing the rope over his shoulder. The little rock bay below can be glimpsed between his legs (*Chapter II*)

11. The view south-westwards from the Svolvær "Goat". The few miles of road on the island can be glimpsed winding along the shore. A bus runs on it to Kabelvaag, the cultural centre of the Lofotens (*Chapter II*)

And had we but known it, this is one of the places where we might have glimpsed that most beautiful of all forest dwellers, the elk. Had we gone on to the tops of the 6,000-foot hills we would certainly have seen reindeer. I recommend Hjerkinn to anyone interested in natural history.

From there we motored through spruce forests, the roads becoming better and better until we were on a real boulevard spanning the lush valley that leads to Trondheim. We camped in the town that night, on the turf roof of an air-raid shelter within sound of working cranes swinging buckets of coal into a ship. We were on the edge of a housing scheme, but even that looked beautiful on such a golden evening, with the fjord patterned with reflections and the low hills bearing their scattered houses like shining pebbles.

Walking into town was rather amusing. For some reason, associated with getting back to nature perhaps, the British mountaineer in foreign parts is apt to show his scorn of the convention of shaving, being unconcerned at the same time with the problem of correct dress. It so happened that our beards were at the scruffy stage, from a distance appearing a growth due to dirt rather than hirsute nature. Also, Scott wore a pair of very short shorts and a green anorak of Eskimo cut. Watson, too, had an anorak, an anorak stained with wild ducks' eggs of two years ago and last year's fish, the whole crowned by a shock of bright red hair. My appearance is comical at the best of times and the less said about it the better.

At any rate, we were greeted in the streets by roars of good-natured laughter and many attempts to interrogate us in English, most of it taken from American film jargon. A more exciting encounter in the back streets was with a galaxy of waving women who were prepared to welcome us with open arms. Fortunately a railway line intervened between us and their advances.

The last straw was when we went to visit Watson senior

B

at the Britannia Hotel, and our entrance was barred by a burly commissionaire, who mistook us, no doubt, for a party of wandering Lapps.   We enjoyed our Pilsener all the more for his disapproval.

Unfortunately this was our last evening united as a party. Tomorrow would see the car heading back south.   A ship called *Lofoten* would bear us northward to the Arctic.

CHAPTER II

Lofoten

A map of Lofoten and the Raftsund is on Page 86

EVERY day a boat leaves Trondheim for the north, calling in at remote fjords, to the Lofoten Islands, to Tromso, and round the North Cape to Kirkenes on the Russian border. Such a jostling match was going on at the quayside that I thought some exciting event must be taking place, such as the arrival of a consignment of polar bears, or perhaps someone had fallen into the harbour. It was no more than the normal process of northward passengers trying to cram aboard an already overcrowded boat—the daily boat to the Arctic.

On the mid-deck it would have been a seething mass—had there been room to seethe. A Clyde steamer at the Glasgow Fair is the only thing I know to compare with it. Fortunately it was a sunny day with the sea a flat calm, and everyone was in the best of spirits, our peculiar appearance contributing not a little to the general smiles.

We made friends quickly, and enjoyed these first few hours, sailing past green headlands where villages clustered below rock slabs polished by the passage of primeval ice streams. Now and again we threaded a way through narrow channels where eider ducks and black guillemots floated. Talking animatedly to a young and very charming schoolteacher called Evileen I nearly missed my first view of an Arctic skua.

Unfortunately the day clouded over before we could take photographs of the many things new to us. At

11

Rörvik we saw our first fish-drying frame, a tall skeleton of bleached wood hung with tenements of swinging cod, mummified to dark and leathery shapes that champed with a dismal clank.   To our astonishment we heard that this was most delicious food, and that an expert can grade eleven different qualities, each being selected for suitability to certain markets.   Spain, Italy, and West Africa are some of the countries which take this food in large quantities. This export trade is a mainstay of the cod-fishing industry in the north.   The fish must be slaughtered immediately they are caught or quality is lowered.

Acting on Adam's advice we had stoked up with bread and provisions before coming aboard the ship, and now we tried our Norwegian in the galley.   It so happened that my first two words of Norwegian were the same as my first two in French.   Years ago on a French train I had wanted boiling water from the dining car to brew up some coffee in the carriage.   The French words for boiling water, I was told, were " Oh should " ; or at least, that is what it sounded like to me.   The magic response in the train kitchen was effective proof of the value of these particular words.   The lesson was not to be lost.   " Cooked vand " (rendered phonetically) are the operative words in Norwegian, and they produced the same desirable result.   We could see that the speed at which we produced our meal was the envy of those unfortunates dependent on an inadequate dining saloon service.

Heaven help the traveller in the north who can't stand noise.   Although we did not know it then, on every Norwegian ship there is an accordion, dancing, and drinking, so you must choose your six by three feet of sleeping space carefully, or you will find yourself caught up in a tango or trampled upon by drunks.   In this land of perpetual daylight, passengers go on and off at all times of night, loud hoots on the siren being the signal for a stop.   We danced for a while, Scott and myself vying for the white hand of Evileen, before stretching out our sleeping-bags

on the draughty upper-deck. It rained, but we let it
rain, rather than join the mass of people lying in corridors,
sitting on stairs, or standing wherever there was cover.

As on other ships, whether in the Mediterranean or the
Clyde, the decks are swabbed at the inhuman hour of
5 a.m. Only once in our travels did we encounter a
gentlemanly sailor who was prepared to swab round us.
He occupies a warm place in my memory.

That night we crossed the magic " circle ". No longer
were we merely travelling. We were in the Arctic, even
if all we could see of it was grey sea and dark mountain
walls on which birch trees managed to cling, and rocks that
would have tested a mountain goat. In the afternoon we
pulled into Bodö, one of the new towns of Norway.

The new Bodö is very smart indeed, almost American
in atmosphere, with its large concrete houses, chromium-
fronted chain stores, and the broadest streets we had seen
in Norway. Great credit should be given for the rapid
reconstruction of these towns, but Bodö seemed a grey
place that wet day, and we came away with an impression
only too reminiscent of Glasgow in its most dismal mood.

The boat, when we got back to it, was like a troopship,
uniformed figures in battledress leaning on every rail.
They were Norwegian recruits, so pleased with army life
that they shouted barrack square commands at each other
and stamped their feet as if they were on the parade-
ground. Some of them even went the length of going
through the motions of rifle drill without rifles. Others
were too drunk to bother. The aqua vita bottle was
circulating with dire effect as we ploughed through choppy
seas, advancing ever closer to our destination, where a dark
fang of rock rose to drizzling cloud. In these conditions of
West Highland grey we sailed into Svolvæer at midnight.

Svolvæer being an Arctic town, the centre of the greatest
cod-fishing in Norway, I expected to find fishermen's
cottages and picturesque-looking sailor types. Instead
there were factory buildings, and taxis on the kerb ; and

though the time was midnight, men and women crowded the harbour as if it were the middle of the day. The women chewed gum, and wore a vivid finery that would not have been out of place in the Bronx. The men were no less smartly dressed, their flowing ties and American cut suits being smarter by far than what I am accustomed to see in Glasgow or London.

This double kick at romance called for drastic action. We hired a taxi—a taxi fitted with radio—and two miles from the town were dumped down at a likely camp spot.

We were tired, and thought all we had to do was put down the tent, get a meal going, and turn into the sleeping-bag. Not expecting high winds we had brought a fairly large bungalow tent. No sooner was it unrolled than it blew out like a balloon, cracking explosively as gust after gust tore at it. Pegs were ripped out of the ground as soon as they were put in, but using ice axes and alpine rope we lashed it down. We even got a meal going inside, but it was a token victory, precariously held, as the tent poles bent like a bow at each furious gust of wind.

It was then Watson appeared with good news. High above us was a tiny hut whose windows had been blown in. It was empty and weatherproof. We bundled our stuff together and staggered uphill. " Staggered " is the word. The steepness of those Lofoten peaks was not appreciated just then. Rather than do two journeys we tried to balance colossal loads up some steep slabby rocks. All went well till the leading man came off and the three of us landed in a cursing heap at the bottom. Dead beat we climbed through the bothy window and fell on the floor, not to rise again for twelve hours.

The outstanding feature that had attracted us to Svolvær was the " Goat ". This is not a mountain in its own right, but a narrow pinnacle that rises 1,000 feet over the town, its crown being twin needles of granite that stick up like a couple of horns. Mist and rain were sweeping across its polished slabs when we looked out. Now and again, immediately above us, we glimpsed its weird outline in dim silhouette. Some half a century ago Cecil Slingsby had made history by climbing it, obtaining the freedom of the town by his feat. The next day we hoped to follow his example, even if not to be fêted as freemen.

Right now the larder needed re-stocking, and to avoid the possibility of a visit from the police, we wanted permission to use the hut. With time on our hands we were able to see and appreciate Svolvær, the capital city of Lofoten. We liked it, for its busy little harbours, the inlets which tell it is a town of islands, the coloured squares of houses with their fish-drying frames gleaming in bursts of sunshine. But above all we liked it for its wide views of mountain and sea, a superb outlook, reminiscent of our own Highland coast, but more splendidly wild. Above us sheer-sided peaks rose to splintered summits. Now we could see the " Goat " properly, and it looked grotesque, its horns curled against flying cumulus clouds.

Shopping was delightful. Before we could buy methylated spirit we had to pass a police interrogation and declare our purpose was not to drink it. Here in Svolvær you can buy ice cream in the streets, English and American magazines in the open bookstall, or catch a bus at hourly intervals to any point in the few miles of road southwards of the town. There are cafés, a picture house, and shops out of all proportion to the population. We understood the need of these shops when we were told that a winter influx of fishermen multiplies the population five-fold, Svolvær getting a fair quota of the 30,000 fishermen and 7,000 boats that crowd the Vest Fjord in search of cod.

The Lofoten season lasts only six weeks, but in that time 55 per cent of Norway's total output of cod is caught. Like the Gulf Stream which promotes it, this wave of spawning fish has never failed the people who depend on it : the men who fish now can claim that their forebears fished the same tide-races of Nordland before there was written history. Certainly for over a thousand years they

have exported cod-liver oil.   We were to hear much about
the fishing industry before we left Norway, for this is the
most fishing-conscious country in the world.

Permission having been received from the owner of the
hut, we retired the possessors of the key.   We would now
be able to dispense with a tedious squirm through a small
window.   It was pleasant around the hut.   Little pockets
of birch trees attracted mealy redpolls and bramblings ; and
growing among the mossy stones were great clumps
of dwarf cornel, buttercups, blue geraniums, saxifrage,
violets, forget-me-nots, little yellow heartsease, and hosts
of commoner things.

Next day in cold and rather misty conditions we climbed
up to the west wall of the " Goat ".   Despite a bold lead
by Scott it rebuffed our first attempt.   The rock was a hard
and slippery granite, reminiscent of the coarse-grained stuff
of the island of Arran.   With difficulty we retraced our
steps over the eighty feet we had climbed and made our
way to the neck from which the " Goat " springs.   Scott
tried the left corner, where the rock was smooth and over-
hung.   The take-off was bad and he did not like it, so
while he came down I investigated the right corner, jugg-
ling on small holds on out-tilted rocks, before making exit
on a sweep of slab that offered a good platform forty feet
up.   Here we assembled, and were faced with a series of
vertical cracks one above the other that led in sixty feet
to an extraordinary niche, a kind of saddle hung in space.
(Plate No. 9.)

The Svolvær face stretched below us, a sheer wall, to
the town.   Immediately above it the rock overhung, and
undoubtedly the route lay up that overhang.   It was certainly going to be exciting.   Scott traversed out to take
a photograph, Watson took anchorage, and I took off, a
real " jug-handle " giving the first lift.   It was an incredible situation—like being on the wall of a skyscraper
looking down on a pygmy landscape.   Below my feet were
the toy houses of the town perched on their little islands.

Hanging out on the bulge, I paused a moment to savour the unique position of my boot heels twixt sky and sea.

It was a shock to relinquish this good hold and realize that a hard bit of climbing lay ahead. A smooth granite slab tapered in a fifty-foot sweep to the point of the higher horn. The only weakness in it was a rounded crack offering small holds for hands and feet. Every move called for considerable care, but one's thoughts were too preoccupied with the next step to concentrate on the long drop below. A last shuffle on toe holds and I was on the ledge immediately under the higher horn, from where I could bring on the others. They were suitably impressed by the downward view.

A short horizontal ledge and we were on the edge of the higher horn, reaching its top by the right-hand skyline shown on the photograph (Plate 9). Now for the famous leap! A few feet down, and perhaps five feet across space was the narrow top of the second horn. Tradition demands that it be jumped. In Slingsby's day our arrival there would have been greeted with a cannon shot. No sooner had I jumped than a different sound floated up to us, the hollow brasses of the town band. We listened. The tune was " The Dead March ". It came from amidst the tombstones of the town cemetery placed a thousand feet below, where a cortège of tiny black matchsticks were assembled. Anyone who fails to make the jump can be assured of immediate interment. This is the only occasion when I have had " the imminence of immediate dissolution " stressed to music.

The jump was easy, though the " take-off " was a trifle unnerving. Now we could relax, and enjoy this sunny eyrie in space. Eastwards, beyond the funeral procession, the chain of mainland peaks stood sharp and clear, like the Torridon coast from the Cuillin hills, only so much wilder and higher, from the gleam of sea-girt glaciers in the south to the blue serrations of fantastic northern peaks.

Below us Svolvæer was spread like a map, tall fish-drying

frames gleaming like the skeletons of prehistoric animals and little fishing boats shuttling back and forth through a maze of islands dotted with houses that looked like so many wooden boxes on the crinkled sea.

It was an historic scene, the scene of our first Commando raid on an enemy-held coast, a bold undertaking delivered on a March morning in 1941 when British fortunes were low and Norwegian morale even lower.

What a thrill it must have been for a disheartened people when the crash of gunfire sounded the death of 18,000 tons of shipping, and British and Norwegian Commandos leapt ashore to stay for $6\frac{1}{2}$ hours, blowing up whale-oil installations and capturing 215 Germans and 10 Quislings. The Germans made history that day by running away. The allies sailed south without a casualty, their number being reinforced by 323 Norwegian volunteers.

It was now a superb afternoon, and we would have dearly loved to stay awhile, and to traverse the main mountain ridge above the town, but we had agreed to meet a Norsk climber of considerable reputation, and time was pressing on. The intention was to go with him to a mountain in the south, Vaagekallen, a peak which rises from the sea in one 3,000-foot bound. We planned to climb it by its most difficult ridge.

After such an exhilarating climb there was a feeling of anti-climax about coming down to earth and taking such prosaic things as bus and taxi to the limit of the southward road. But we were soon enchanted by the crossing of a little pass into a flower-covered corrie.

Above us rose our mountain, its jagged summit an edge of living copper that turned to fire as the sun dipped towards the Arctic Ocean. " Tonight will be very beautiful on the tops," said Olsen. We thought so too, but we were tired, and the climb was reputedly difficult ; and anyhow, there would be plenty of other nights to witness the fantastic splendours of mountain and ocean ablaze with fiery light. Little did we know as we crawled into our sleeping-bags that we were missing the only chance of a perfect night that we were to have.

The morning broke dull, and from the ridge marking the beginning of our climb we saw the tall islands being blotted out one by one by veils discharging from an advancing wall of steel-grey cloud. We were certainly going to get wet.

We roped up and started an abominable climb, Olsen leading me at a furious pace. Scott and Watson wisely climbed on a second rope. We were on an exposed hanging garden rather than a rock face, moss and turf providing precarious holds for fingers and ice-axe blade. More often than not the rope was a tangled ball between us, threatening to catch on every protuberance, for Olsen gave no thought at all to it.

Not wishing to carp, I said nothing, but took opportunity to unravel it as he struggled in a cleft immediately above me. Suddenly there was a shout and the rasp of loosening rock. I had no anchorage on the mountain but swung myself out of the line of fire, dropping the tangled rope and grasping the end nearest to Olsen in case he came off. The loosened blocks smashed down on the place where I had been standing, cutting the rope in three places. Luckily the others were out of danger.

Above that cleft Olsen indicated that he expected trouble. The mountain was rent by a square-sided cleft sixty feet high, the first bit of clean rock we had seen on this peak. The first part was a straightforward chimney, but thirty feet up he asked me if I would join him for combined tactics. It was far from being a safe place, for I was precariously placed and powerless to hold him in event of a slip. With my hand supporting his foot on a tiny wrinkle, he tried to reach a hand-hold a long way out on the far wall of the cleft. It was a delicate move, his body being thrown out of balance by the verticality of the wall. He made it, and wrestled strenuously above with a great block that barred exit from the cleft.

He was up just in time.   Down came the rain, hissing down the rocks, making conditions greasy for Scott and Watson, who wisely tied themselves on to our rope.   The top was only three hundred feet above us, but after one more difficult section, Olsen decided to give the mountain best.   Descent from the top would take six hours at least, he said, and he was not very sure of the route.   In view of this we fixed rope slings and double-roped the difficult sections of the downward route.   The chief interest of the descent was in large patches of rose-pink snow, a pheno-menon due to vegetable dye.

Luckily there had been time to spare in the morning before leaving, and we had boiled a pot of water into which we put dried soup, carrots, and turnips, wrapping it up in my sleeping-bag before departure.   It was now perfectly cooked and required only five minutes on the stove to put us right with the world.   This improvised hay-box method of cookery deserves to be better known.   Such things as rice and porridge can be cooked to perfection this way.

Having tried our hands on the " Goat " and Vaagakallen, the time had now come to face the problem of getting into wilder territory.   The Raftsund was the place.   But with-out a boat of our own, the carrying out of a mountaineering project into its sea narrows seemed fraught with difficulties. Its peaks are reputed to give the finest climbing in the Lofotens, with endless possibilities of new ascents.   The first move was clearly to go back to the hut at Svolvær, and buy in a store of provisions so that we could promote things in our own interest.

The weather could hardly have been worse.   Rain showered over our sleeping-bags, and a coat fastened over the window bellied like a sail, blowing in time after time, covering us with spray.   Fortunately, Norwegian hospit-ality came to the rescue, relieving the problem of bed-sores from too much lying in sleeping-bags.   First, with Magnar Pettersen, a little fellow with sandy-coloured hair and a pair of the bluest eyes I have ever seen.   Magnar is a bachelor, and he took us to his rooms, the rooms of a scholar and mountaineer. Above his crammed bookcase were his ice-axe, rifle and shotgun, and certificates in Norwegian and English commending his bravery in the Second World War.

He operated a wireless receiving set during the occupation, and for a time assisted English and Allied troops to escape through the mountains of north Norway into Sweden. Magnar soon put us right on most of the things we wanted to know. If we chose our day we could get a milk-marketing-board boat to the Raftsund. We would certainly get the loan of a small boat to take us to a camping site. Bread would be baked for us by the nearest crofters. Potatoes could be had for the asking, and we could catch our own fish. As for getting back. " Just row out and stop any passing boat," we were told ; a new method of using the thumb.

And while we waited for the boat we were entertained by the Mosbyes, a delightful family, who, knowing we were not too comfortable in the bothy, prevented us from going by providing tea every time we made a move to go. It was a tactful way of prolonging a visit that stretched to over eight hours, during which time the conversation never flagged.

Mr. Mosbye is manager of an important oil company, and knows Norway from end to end. He is also a keen skier and sportsman, with a love for his country that was inspiring. He told me much of what I wanted to know.

Taxation, for example. It is higher in Norway than in Britain, though the wage for an average working man is £7 10s. per week. As for fishermen's earnings in Svolvær, one owner earned 350,000 kroner in three weeks. (1 krone equals one shilling.) The industry is so well organized today that it was difficult to buy fish in the town. Fish meal, fish oil, fish drying, deep freezing, even plastics, are absorbing all the available fish.

We spoke of Russia and its frontier with Norway at Kirkenes. It used to be a tourist attraction to go to the border and take photos looking into what used to be Finland but is now the Iron Curtain. The Russians didn't like it and made formal protest, so nowadays cameras may not be pointed at the line of little barrels marking the " Curtain ".

No one on the Russian side ever speaks to anyone on the Norwegian side, even when they come down to fish the river that is common property. People who were friends before the occupation no longer speak, and if an animal should cross the border, its reinstatement must go through the Kremlin.

If a Norwegian official wants to speak with a Russian official, he must hoist a flag on the frontier, where he will be met by his counterpart. Come rain or the snows of winter they must do their talking under the sky, for the Russians have considered, and rejected (after two years' thought), the proposal to build a shelter.

Yet despite obvious restrictions on liberty, there are more Communists in Kirkenes and the surrounding district than in any other part of Norway. It seems a mad bit of world.

For us—regarded as mad in a different kind of way—the time had come to catch the milk boat.

CHAPTER III

The Raftsund

EMIL OLSEN, who has been with us on Vaagekallen, was supposed to be coming with us, but we were hardly surprised when he failed to appear. It was a coarse day, too wet and cold for crouching on the deck of a small fishing craft that was the milk boat, but at last we ran under the lee of Store Molla to shelter by its green flanks, where peat stacks and little squares of cultivation gave it a Scottish appearance.

The west wall of the Oyhelle Sund was a startling contrast. Here the crags rose in black sheets smooth as boilerplates, enclosing ragged snow banners and long gullies. We might have been looking into the north-east corrie of Ben Nevis, except that these crags were so much fiercer. Rumour had it that these were gabbro peaks. We did not need to be geologists to see that we were looking at an objectionable type of granite, the type of coarse-grained stuff that gives foothold to every kind of moss and lichen but very little to the climber. Expecting gabbro, the cleanest and roughest climbing rock known to mountaineers, we were disappointed. But not for long. Suddenly, above the swirl of rain clouds we saw Rulten, such a thrust of naked rock that we were silenced. Any rock structure that can produce such a mountain has everything to recommend it. No wonder its fierce crest had such a reputation. Whatever happened now or later we would need to try our hands on its 3,000-foot granite walls.

The Oyhelle Sund, through which we were steaming, is a shallow straight of such wonderfully clear water that we looked through a natural aquarium to the pebbles and golden weed of the sea floor. Great starfish lay on the bottom, and jellyfish like pink balloons floated swiftly past. The darting bodies of large cod and saithe promised that we would not lack fish.

Magnar had told us to get off the boat at Slôthollmen, where we would meet a man from the Raftsund who came daily to collect papers and mail. He was right. Despite the rough day, Mr. Dahl was there, a friendly little man full of good humour, who not only rowed us to our destination, but invited us to his house for anything we required in the way of potatoes, milk, and eggs. Bread would be baked for us as required.

Though it was a poor night, we were delighted with our camp spot. We were on the edge of the sound, with rock peaks rising straight behind us. Little inlets and lagoons invited exploration, and groves of birch trees promised interesting things in the way of birds. The croft, half a mile away, was the nearest habitation. All we needed was some decent weather.

It came in the morning, like a day in spring in the Highlands, the peaks streaming with mist, rock slabs and snowfields glistening, the transparent green sea reflecting the birch groves on its edge. We set off on reconnaissance, going northward to a deep glen cutting into a peak called the Store Trolltind. At eight hundred feet it was a wintry world. Ice sheeted the hill lochs and steep snow walls depended from the mountain flanks. Among the clouds we caught glimpses of dark pinnacles and spiky ridges, remote as Alpine summits. We were rather proud of the fact that though we knew nothing of the mountain, and had a most inadequate map, we nevertheless selected the correct route to the summit. But we did not climb it that day.

Instead, we plumped for a peak that promised views into

2. Destination, the Raftsund, the great peaks rising in sheer rock from the narrow waters of this fierce sound (*Chapter III*)

13. Camp at Korsnes. On the left is the island of Store Molla, enclosing the narrow waters of the Oyhelle Sund. A dense tangle of dwarf birches covers the headland in the middle distance (*Chapter III*)

14. The camp at Korsnes and the peak of the Rorhoptind, climbed by the party. The tent is on a little promontory, backed by dwarf birches and crags (*Chapter III*

15. Much bad weather curtailed climbing activities, but many fish were caught, providing good sport. Adam Watson guts some coal-fish, the commonest summer fish in these coastal waters (*Chapter III*)

16. Lofoten vegetation, being ungrazed, is often a jungle of tall ferns covering slippery boulders. Sometimes they grow as tall as a man, making walking a toil (*Chapter III*)

17. Trakta. Bad weather foiled our hopes on this fine mountain (*Chapter III*)

18. Looking north-east from a 4,000-foot peak above Narvik to the mountains of Swedish Lapland, the highest peaks in the Arctic (*Chapter IV*)

19. Lyngen Fjord (*Chapter IV*)

20. (above) The summit of Jaeggevarre, 6,220 feet, and the compelling range of the Lakselvtinder, where hosts of mountaineering problems still await solution (*Chapter IV*)

21. (below) The "Cuillin-like" summits of the Jaegervandstind seen from the most northerly point of Jaeggevarre. The problem of where to climb next was solved for us when we saw this welter of rock peaks and hanging glaciers (*Chapter IV*)

22. The camp at Lyngen Fjord and the scattered crofts of this remote peninsula. The peaks in the background reach a height of over 5,000 feet. Crofting and fishing are the main livelihoods of the people (*Chapter IV*)

23. The glacier of the Jaegervandstind. This was an extremely broken glacier, heavily crevassed, rising steeply for over a thousand feet to a great amphitheatre from which the peaks rose in rock ribs to narrow summits (*Chapter IV*)

the wildest fjord in Norway, the Trollfjord, a weird slash
of black water cutting a ravine between vertical rock walls.
It was an impressive sight. But beyond it was a still wilder
scene, the Trollfjordvand, an Arctic waste of frozen water
hemmed between 3,000-foot walls. From its narrow shores
the glaciers rose between black crags. Now and then we
glimpsed the bulge of overhangs and tilted pinnacle edges.
No wonder such a menacing place was named the abode of
Trolls, Norwegian equivalents to the Kelpies of Scotland,
or the Ferlie Mor (Grey Man) of Ben Macdhui.

In these surroundings, much to our surprise, we saw a
miniature power scheme in the process of construction.
From this source of power the scattered houses of the
adjacent islands are to get electricity. There is no getting
away from progress in this land of Norway.

Our peaklet had given some hardish rock climbing. We
did not return to camp empty-handed. Two loaves warm
from the oven, and six pints of milk were waiting for us
at the croft—thick creamy milk that had the effect of good
beer. This place was such a tiny oasis in a wilderness of
rock we wondered how these people lived. We learned
much about them before we left the Lofotens.

The paucity of bird life was surprising. All we had
seen that day were hoodie crows, some flocks of twites,
fieldfares, willow grouse, a few magpies, wheatears, house
sparrows, a wren, meadow and tree pipits, and a few water
birds such as guillemots, Arctic terns, cormorants, and
mergansers. The only wading birds seemed to be sandpipers, redshanks, and oyster-catchers. We had expected
much more. In fact, our Lofoten list came to only thirty-
five species, but it included white-tailed eagle and golden
eagle. After the tundra country it was a disappointment.

The willow grouse were particularly interesting. These
white-winged birds crow and shout like our own red grouse.
It is when they fly it is apparent that they are a different
species, more like the white-winged ptarmigan we see in
summer on the Scottish hills. The admonition " go back,

go back " might be slightly harsher in note than our own red grouse. The really interesting thing about the willow grouse is that in winter it turns white, though at all seasons it remains a bird of the scrub woods.

Clouds and intermittent rain foiled our mountain plans for the following day, but it did not prevent us fishing the aquarium-like waters of the sound. Mr. Dahl obligingly lent us his boat and tackle, and in no time we were hauling in the fish, the heaviest being a 23-lb. saithe. From out on the sound we obtained a better idea of the peaks clustering so closely above us. The best of these was a shapely peak identified as the main summit of the Rorhoptinder, 3,610 feet. There and then we decided to go for it, bad weather or no.

But it was 10 p.m. before we left. The peak lay southward of us, above a narrow inland water called the Rorhopvatn. In our innocence we thought we could walk along the shore and follow up a small glacier we had seen from the sea. A steep tangle of birches and rocks rent by gullies forced us higher, to an undulating moor which led in hard walking to a granite wall for all the world like the horrible vegetatious face of Cioch na Oighe of the island of Arran.

The prospect of contouring that face was no more alluring than the only alternative—to go down to lake level. Realizing what we were in for, we committed ourselves to the line of least resistance on the face. The walls were greasy, mossy and wet, but we made good progress and enjoyed the work. So far we had climbed unroped, but the exposure of an abyss forced us to don the rope and try some sporting climbing of the chimney and slab variety. With considerable pleasure we saw we were now close to the glacier, separated from it by a wall of treacherous-looking slabs.

First it meant a descent of a mossy wall, almost devoid of handhold, but suitable for jamming the axe pick. Once down this an easy ledge provided a narrow gangway to a small tree to which a rope belay could be fixed. All this took time, but we were jubilant, and agreed that these were superlative little mountains.

The snow at our feet reached steeply to the coal-black loch. Above it, on the opposite shore, rose a face like Aonach Dubh of Glencoe, sloping back to a shallow corrie where mist swirled round some black pinnacles.

Climbing a delightful little rock rib for several hundred feet, we were on the glacier, and soon kicking and cutting steps up a gully leading to the true ridge of the mountain. Confined by its enclosing walls, it was a superb moment when we stepped over the crest and looked down on a pearly sea silhouetted with craggy islands and skerries. At the early hour of two in the morning, the luminous sky and dotted islands had the enchanted quality of a fairy tale.

We followed a snow cornice, contouring under the summit crag until two hundred feet above us was the narrow point of the summit. It was bitterly cold up there, but the climbing was strenuous and warming, and our only regret was the mist which prevented proper views of the Alpine ridges on both sides of us.

Having gone up the north side of the mountain we examined the south face. It was impressive ; great granite slabs cut by a snow couloir of imposing steepness. We thought of a glissade at first, but the angle was too fierce and the consequences of mistake too serious. Cutting and kicking and rock scrambling we were soon in an easier gully and glissaded merrily for over a thousand feet to the corrie floor, to where the stream emerged from the gorge walls. A shaft of sunlight breaking through for a brief moment illuminated our spirits as well as the mountain walls.

Here we made a mistake by trying to contour to the north. The ground looked easier than the gorge-floor, and we made good speed at first, forcing our way through a tangle of birches. Suddenly we were faced with a " cut-off ", a cliff so steep that we could not see the bottom of

it. Much climbing and contouring brought us to the stage
when each man thought the other was responsible for such
a crazy choice of route. At last we were forced to loop
the rope round a birch tree and slide down 50 feet of
slimy wall to a stance.

If we knew little about Lofoten vegetation then we were
to discover a lot more inside the next hour or two. Birches
and ferns are the bane of mountaineering in the Raftsund.
It is not just a question of having to force a way through
at every step. The really ugly part is that the vegetation
acts as a screen for great holes and boulders, so that one
has to be on the alert all the time. It is really wonderful
country for breaking a leg. Tempers were more than a
little raw by the time we pushed through to the seashore
to begin the long boulder-hop back to camp. The sun was
shining and it looked like being a fine day as we turned
in to our sleeping-bags at an hour when most business
people are rushing to catch the morning train.

It was 3 p.m. when we rose to boil up a pot of sea-water
and drop our fish into it. This is the way to cook saithe
or cod. Five minutes and it is ready. With some new
potatoes one could hardly wish for anything better. Our
meals took no regard to the clock. In a land of perpetual
daylight time doesn't matter. The weather does, for we
had discovered that these little peaks are too exacting for
enjoyment when moss and lichen make each hand and
foothold a test of slippery adhesion.

Right now it looked like being another drizzly day, and
we were content to await developments by trying a cast
in the sound. This time, however, we caught only a 12-lb.
pollack and a 2-lb. cod.

That night as we lay in our sleeping-bags we were set
wondering by some unusual sounds : grunts, squeals, and
barks. In a land where there is no summer darkness it
could hardly be badgers. After a short silence it broke
out again. Our thoughts were now on otters or wildcats.
Stealthily we crawled out, following the sounds to their

source among trees and rocks. It was a fox, or more probably foxes. Unless we had seen them we would not have
credited that these beasts could make such sounds.

Speaking of this to a crofter later, he showed no surprise.
The place was infested with foxes, he said, and their main
food was willow grouse. He had no enmity to the beast
at all, despite the fact that he saw them repeatedly around
his house. As he had hens and a few sheep, I could only
conclude that the fox in Lofoten is a better behaved animal
than is its counterpart in Britain.

The following day was Sunday, and as it was still raining
we had a long lie-in. The weather never looked less
promising. A walk to the farm galvanized us into action.
There was a boat leaving in one hour for Svolvæer and
we could have a lift.

We were going to test the theory that the farther north
you go in the Arctic the better becomes the weather. The
highest peaks in Arctic Norway were at Lyngen, north of
Tromso. We could go there and see if we could find clear
skies and glimpse the midnight sun that we had heard so
much about.

Our main fear as we sailed down the Raftsund was that
the weather was not going to wait until we got to Lyngen.
The clouds were lifting from peak after peak and patches
of blue sky were spreading in all directions.

CHAPTER IV

Jaeggevarre—"The Mont Blanc of the North"

A map of Lyngen is on Page 87

FATE determined things for us at Svolvær. There was a boat for Narvik due to leave at midnight, and we bundled our gear aboard, trying hard not to look at the mountain peaks whose shoulders were being gilded one after another with the low light of a golden sun. We had some eggs and made an omelette, screening the primus from the sharp eyes of the crew, who were obliged to take disciplinary action against this breach of convention if it came to their notice.

The whole wall of the Raftsund was clear when we sailed, a mountaineer's dream of purple and gold, each shattered peak a silhouette against the blaze of the midnight sun. In the amazing visibility following the rains, the air had a translucence vanquishing space. Southward, as far as the eye could see, were rock needles sharp as pencil strokes, island peaks of Landegode and Moskenes.

One could not go to sleep on such a night. By our impatience we had lost our chance ashore of the most colourful night any of us are ever likely to see. We were determined not to miss the highlights of a sail which brought new peaks continually within our vision—from the pinnacled snows of Moisalen and the Blue Mountains, to the first starboard glimpse of a fantastic mountain—Stedtind.

Slingsby called it " the ugliest mountain in the world ",

also, " the most unique natural obelisk in the world, rising
in one single piece of stone to a height of 5,000 feet above
the blue fjord ". A Norwegian climber called it " a mar-
vellous castle of silver-grey granite ". We drew ever
closer to an anvil peak, so square-sided it was hard to
believe that it was climbable. A ribbon of snow of
celestial delicacy hung on its topmost crest. Slingsby, fired
by the inaccessibility of that crest, tried to reach it in
1904, but was beaten only five hundred feet from the
summit by two crags barring the only rock *arête* to the
final " obelisk ".

That same summer an attack was made by an Alpine
Club party containing the great names of Priestman, Carr,
and Ouston. They were unsuccessful. This is what they
said of it : " From the Stedfjorden we saw the horrifying
monster rising with its horizontally cut summit in infernal
majesty over 5,000 feet almost vertically from the fjord.
In front of this mountain those who say that the Matterhorn
is ugly would change their adjective to beautiful when
comparing the two."

Thanks to the encouragement of Slingsby, the peak was
climbed successfully in 1910 by Norwegians, and how
difficult it was is shown by the fact that even with rock-
climbing standards as they are today, the ascent still ranks
as severe, the key to the climb being a delicate hand
traverse to a most sensational crack. This is not the only
route now. The slabs which Slingsby and other pioneers
thought so impossible have been climbed by mechanized
methods of ring spikes and rope engineering. Only by
the utmost enterprise in a land of perpetual daylight are
such long and arduous routes possible. It is appropriate
that the man who made them, Arne Naess, has since distinguished himself in the high Himalayas by leading his
Norwegian party to the top of Tirich Mir, 25,263 feet.

Not until our brains and eyes were befuddled with a
never-ending succession of rock peaks did we crawl into
our sleeping-bags on the draughty deck. From a cavern

of darkness within the warm down I was stirred to wakefulness by the ticket collector. It was 9 a.m. The light
was blindingly brilliant, and we were almost in Narvik.
We were sailing close to a wooded shore from which shot
a dazzlingly bright snow peak, curved against a sky of
almost Tibetan blue, pale and brittle rather than intensely
dark. The air was crisp with cold.

On such a peaceful morning it was hard to believe that
this was the historic scene of so much battle and blood.
Into this fjord H.M.S. *Warspite* had sailed in 1940, blast-
ing the Germans, sinking several destroyers and chasing
another three up a side fjord until they ran aground. The
Germans were arresting people for smiling that day. You
are still a pretty big man in Norway if you are a Britisher.

Narvik treated us well. I went into a shop to buy
paraffin and was promptly toasted in " finspirit ", a swig
from the communal bottle almost laying me low. The
stairs felt a long way off as I made careful descent. Much
reconstruction on houses and streets was going on, and we
were impressed by the fine new town that was being
created, a town of infinitely more charm than modern
Bodö.

From Narvik our plan was to go north by long-distance
bus to Lyngen Fjord. But as usual when we wanted to
go anywhere in the north, the operative time of departure
of the vehicle was midnight. That gave us nine hours
to kill—not sufficient to journey to the " Sleeping Queen "
and climb its 5,000-foot top, but sufficient to reach a peak
about the height of Ben Nevis above the town.

It did not look much of a peak, but it turned out to be
quite a mountain. The route we took led us to a clearing
in the hillside where trees had been cut to make the local
ski-jump, a gigantic scaffolding of pine logs affording scope
to the most suicidal of ski-jumpers. If you imagine coming
off the top of a city building on skis you will have a fairly
accurate idea of the " take-off " for the jump.

The path wound delightfully from here, through birch

scrub and flower-covered turf to a rocky corrie. Family parties out for the day were dotted about the slopes. Their Mecca was a flagstaff on the first top at about 3,000 feet, a point commanding a wide view of blue fjords, and mountains stretching from Sweden into Finnmark.

Above this, the ridge swept to a snowy flank curving in a horseshoe of crags to a blunt summit hung with cornices. The air up here was pleasantly cool and we climbed in anticipation of outstanding views. The low sun was already topping the mountain landscape with gold, deepening the valleys with shadow. Scattered among the rocks were splashes of vivid purple saxifrage, the biggest and most splendid clusters we had ever seen.

There was a glorious sense of peace and freedom up here. We looked across to Swedish Lapland, to the unbroken snows of Kebnekaise and its neighbours, the highest peaks in the Arctic, a bare and sparsely inhabited landscape. Beyond the twistings of fjords and dark sea were the Lofotens, their mountain edges blurred with haze. Northward the scene was of an empty land, of mountains rising on a gaunt horizon. It looked as if we were heading towards a sombre land.

We found it was an illusion. The bus jolted us through a country that was far from sombre. Our kit piled on the roof of this northward-bound vehicle, we vibrated and twisted a way through an enchanting series of little passes, climbing over ridges, threading through woods and lakes, past little hamlets tucked away in folds of the hills.

Always there was something to see, glimpses across new fjords, or the Alpen-glow of snow peaks reflected in the still waters of a lake. We were in the finest elk country in Norway, a country of birch trees, with groves of spruce and pine. It was frostily cold, and now and then we ran into hanging masses of dense mist. Occasionally we stopped at wayside houses for coffee. We were glad when sunlight filled the valleys and the pale sky had deepened to blue.

Just after 7 a.m. we drew up to a cross-roads and were

told this was as far as we could go. In nine hours we would be able to pick up another vehicle, meantime we could cool our heels. We decided to camp and snatch some sleep. A flat stretch of green was right to hand and there were houses where we could get water for a meal when we wanted it.

We pitched camp and tried to sleep. It was not very successful. No sooner were we relaxed and dozing when there was a jangling of bells from an animal that did its best to wrap itself round the guy-ropes. Then we became aware of flies and mosquitoes. We were determined to sleep and jammed our eyes tight shut, ignoring their zooming. But the heat inside a closed sleeping-bag was overpowering, and we were irritated continually by animals or humans moving about. By mid-day we gave up, more tired than when we had gone to bed.

The map of Lyngen tells you very little. No glaciers are marked, the contouring is sketchy, and the mountain streams are indefinite. The scale is four miles to one inch, admirably suited to this kind of economy of detail. But the cartographers have had the goodness to insert the highest peak, Jaeggevarre, Slingsby's " Mont Blanc of the North ", height 6,109 feet, and as the nearest place to it on our map seemed to be Forladt, we pointed it out to the bus conductor and that was where he ushered us out.

This moment should have been one of jubilation. Instead there were long faces in the party. Jaeggevarre, or what little we could see of it, seemed an imposter, 6,000 feet of rounded hump. After the Lofotens the fjord seemed a deep and dismal place, not helped by dull overhanging cloud. Moreover, half the village had accompanied us to camp and seemed reluctant to go away. They were small Lapp types, inquisitive rather than friendly, quite unlike other Norwegians we had met.

Knowing that mountains—even rounded ones—are a cure for the blues, we set off at once for the peak, determined to climb through the night. The time was

8.40 p.m., and in two hours' walking through birches, past an uninhabited Lapp shelter, we had opportunity to revise our ideas. What had appeared from camp as a rounded hump was now apparent as a great ice-cap overhanging a face of unprepossessing cliff. From the foot of it we could see the tumble of *séracs* belonging to an abnormally low glacier. Getting onto the glacier was not going to be the walk-over we had imagined.

We examined the map, looking in vain for some of these features. Although we did not know it then, even the true top of the mountain was wrongly marked. Not managing to make very much of streams that did not orient, and peaks that were not even marked, we decided we would contour direct through birches on our north flank, to a steep face split by rock gullies. From the top of this we might by-pass the glacier and strike a ridge to the summit.

It was a blunder, but an interesting blunder. The scrub was dense and the boulders trying before we struck rock. Mosquitoes plagued us, buzzing round, stinging us on the hands as we scrambled from one rock gully to another. They were still with us at four thousand feet, borne up no doubt by blasts of hot air that struck us from time to time.

Suddenly we saw the folly of our way. From the crest of our ridge Jaeggevarre came into view, aglow with rich light. Like marzipan on a cake, its snow dome flowed over an edge of cliffs, chocolate-coloured in the warmth of the midnight sun. On a level with our own height was a line of shadow as cold as winter. Even as we watched, the summit glow changed to copper and a slow-burning, lingering fire.

Our false peak had placed us in an ideal position for reconnaissance of the great south-east face before us. Breaching the ice-cap where it overflowed the rocks was going to be the obvious difficulty, and we picked out a rock rib connecting to a point which appeared safe from possible

avalanche.   This, if it could be climbed, would land us on
a top north of what we thought was the main summit.
In fact, the main summit is separated by a col and 1,500 feet
of rise from that shown on the map.

The first thing was to get safely down to the glacier by
the steep snow and rocks at our feet, and we took it carefully.
Down there the snow was iron hard and we surveyed our
hemmed-in position gleefully, casting our eyes upwards to
the unknown, where great ribs of gabbro leapt to the
glistening ice-cap.

A sharp bout of step-cutting and rock scrambling, a
traverse, and we were at the foot of our rock rib, out of
shadow, and into the morning sparkle of red-grey rock,
ice, and blue sky.   At our side an ice fall plunged like a
frozen fountain, pinnacles glistening.

At once we struck the kind of climbing we like best,
mixed rock and snow such as we get on the Nevis ridges
in spring-time.   The climbing was steep, yet we could
move together, except where vertical sections intervened.
The ice-cap was bigger and steeper than we thought, but
so well frozen it was a joy to cut steps up it and step
onto the top at 6.30 a.m. thinking the summit was in the
bag.

It was not, but we had no thought of that just then.
Around us was a welter of peaks, fjords, and islands.   We
felt that this must have been what the Scottish Highlands
were like in the ice age, with glaciers flowing into the glens,
ice fields shining on the tops, and long ridges of naked rock
soaring up from the depths of blue fjords.   Beyond the
press of snow cornices and spiky gabbro, stretching into
space, was the snow-flecked tundra of Finnmark and
Swedish Lapland, reaching into Finland itself—a lonely,
colourless land of mosquito-ridden bogs and lakes, inhabited
by countless hosts of wading birds and wild ducks—a land
bitingly cold in winter.   In this visibility the Narvik peaks
looked astonishingly near, and northward we could see
every wrinkle of the Oksfjordjokel, which is the only glacier

remaining in Norway which flows from mountain tops to calve its icebergs into the fjord.

But the range that excited us most was a kind of Cuillin ridge of sharp peaks rising immediately in front of us, part of the Lyngen peninsula. According to the map they were the Jaegervandstinder. The problem of where to go next was solved for us.

Now we could see the summit of our peak and a white bird that may have been a snowy owl flapping over it. We wished we were that bird. It was a crushing experience to have to lose height, climb up to the summit marked as the highest point on the map, and find ahead of us a top unmistakably higher. To reach it meant a drop of a thousand feet to a col from which rose a rounded dome sliced sheer at one end where the great ice-cap lunged over cliff, ready to avalanche.

We were rather tired by now, and rested here awhile, basking in warmth and eating our last sandwich. The imprint of recent footprints was interesting. We had discovered roughly three sets of them on top of the north-east peak, and they seemed to be heading for the main summit. We followed them, climbing over crevasses and undulations of firm snow, to reach the summit at 9 a.m. Taking off the rope each of us went for a wander.

I went to the edge of the ice, to look down on the green waters of a glacier lake—the Fugledalsvatn. Times have changed since Slingsby wrote so romantically of its glacier snout reaching far into its dark waters. The glacier has receded quite a bit since then. This is what Slingsby says : " See those huge black ice-capped precipices of Jekkevarre. See below them that large secondary glacier or glacier remains, probably the best example of its kind in Europe. See, too, how far its snout projects into the dark waters of that weird Fugledalsvatn, and tell me if you can, where this scene has a rival ! " I could think of none.

The compelling range of mountains from here was the Lakselvtinder. They seemed to rise from the base of our mountain, sending up ridge after ridge from a glacier torn in crevassed folds, to narrow summits sharp as aiguilles. Here was a range offering some of the finest mountaineering we had ever imagined. The possibilities of new routes, even new ascents, urged us to scrap our plans for the Jaegervandstind and go to this group instead.

Meantime there was plenty of mountaineering ahead of us. The mysterious footsteps seemed to retrace their way over the north peak. We had hoped they might lead us to an easy way down. We decided to go back to the col between us and the north peak, climb up for a bit, then try a route down from a point on the south-east face of the north peak. We thought we could detect a likely looking rib.

It proved a myth. An abominably steep snow couloir grooved by avalanche runnels led from the ice-cap, disappearing out of sight after two thousand feet. The alternative was a rock rib beginning under an overhanging snow cornice. A large fragment of ice-cap falling like a thunder-clap down the precipice of the main peak implanted a feeling of caution. We slashed down the cornice and took to the rocks, following a rather delicate line to join the couloir at a point where it was screened from the threat of direct avalanche.

The snow slope was so steep that we had to face inward, each step demanding several kicks of the boot. A rock face immediately below impressed the need for care. We were glad to get to it and descend steep slabs leading to a snowy gully containing some rock pitches. By an amazing stroke of luck our route was the only way through the massed pinnacles of a huge ice fall overhanging the crags on our south flank.

If we were tired we had not noticed it in the excitement. Below us was level glacier and bare ice that kept us on the alert for another hour or more. Now we could relax, our limbs felt sluggish, and the sliding stones of the moraine were annoying.

Then we heard whistles. Bearing down on us fast was a pair of bearded climbers. Their curiosity in this remote place was as thoroughly aroused as ours. There was a mutual cry of recognition as Adam recognized Dick Brown of Sheffield, whom he had met in the Lofotens the previous year. We settled down to have a chat and get an explanation of the footsteps we had seen.

Dick and his companion, Nobby Clarke of Birmingham, were members of a large mountaineering and scientific expedition based at a Lyngen schoolhouse. Right now they had a camp in the birch woods two miles from where we were sitting, and they were engaged in mapping the complications of Jaeggevarre and learning something of the movements of its glaciers. Various members of the party had been on the mountain, a party going up by a rib on the north peak, returning by a snow gully on the same face.

Meantime they produced a bag of raisins and invited us to partake of some. They will never know what an effort it cost us to refuse more than just a few. Back in their camp we did not need pressing to have a cup of sweet coffee, and under its influence we leapt across the various streams between us and camp. The finale of the day was a tonguing from a crofter for walking over his hayfield.

The time was 11 p.m., so the peak had taken over twenty-three hours and given us some first-rate mountaineering. What matter if it had been done on a ration of three slices of bread and four sweets per man. It was unfortunate, though, that the sausages on which our thoughts had been fastened for so many hours were sour and had reluctantly to be tossed into the fjord. We made a soup, but before it was ready, heads were nodding in sleep, and we knew little for the next twelve hours.

It is perhaps worth mentioning that the first ascent of this mountain was in 1897 by G. Hastings and H. Wooley. By 1898 three other ascents had been made, two of them by Wooley and one by Mrs. Main and the Imbodens. No ascent was made for the next twenty-five years. Unless the Germans climbed the mountain during the occupation it is unlikely that more than a dozen ascents have been made all told. Our routes appear to be new ones.

4. The glacier under which we bivouacked for the ascent of the Jaegervandstind
(*Chapter V*)

26. The "Crux" of this climb was a delicate balancing movement on small holds. Scott is about to make the last move. His rope hangs across the gap.

25. A problem on the Jaegervanstind was to surmount a deep gap where a great cut in the ridge occurred. Scott has descended into the gap and has climbed forty feet up the far wall.

(*Chapter V*)

27. The move made, he surmounts the last few feet to a stance, there to await the arrival of Watson and the Author.

28. Attaining the summit meant a cautious sidle along this narrow ledge, then out over an overhang on the left with a thousand-foot drop below. Forty feet of steep climbing led on to the summit.

29. Jaeggevarre, 6,220 feet, the highest peak in Arctic Norway, its ice-cap flowing over gabbro cliffs. The main peak can be glimpsed on the left. A traverse of its three summits gave 23 hours of hard mountaineering with superlative views over Finnmark and Swedish Lapland (*Chapter V*)

30. Descent from the Trolltind, looking south over the Stortind to Jaeggevarre, whose ice-cap over-tops everything else in view (*Chapter V*)

31. After a washout at the upper bivouac, with the tent repaired and our clothing hanging out to dry (*Chapter V*)

32. The " Lapp of Luxury ". This Lapland woman wanted money because the author took her picture. A tarpaulin covering a wooden frame is the home of the mother and child. The tribe had an economy founded not entirely on reindeer, but with the sideline of selling trinkets to tourists (*Chapter V*)

33. Papa Lapp confines his activities to watching the baby, while his wife tries to dispose of a few trinkets and items of knitwear. It must be admitted that the goods were sold at bargain prices (*Chapter V*)

54. Climbing types from Scotland and the Midlands on the boat from Kjosen Fjord. Watson and Scott are second and third respectively from the left. The others are members of the Oread Mountaineering Club who spent two months climbing in the Lyngen area, making some fine ascent and preparing the most comprehensive exploration of the whole area. (Chap. VI)

Bivouac on the Jaegervandstind

THE rival claims of the Lakselvtinder were ruled out when we discovered that the only access was by an infrequent boat service. Accordingly we made plans to catch the afternoon bus northward to Lyngseidet. With great thoroughness we packed everything, leaving only the essentials for a meal. The plans were made but the coffee wasn't when the bus passed, making us look a bit foolish. We scrambled wildly to intercept it, but there was nothing doing.

All was not yet lost. There was a military camp nearby, a handful of men, but they had a lorry, and if we knew anything about soldiers it was likely they would be heading for the high spots when their day was done. It was worth paying them a visit. Yes, we could get a lift. No nonsense here about not giving lifts to civilians. Our baggage was duly picked up and we headed north. They were a cheery crowd. One of them was a young hero who had set up a new record on the Narvik ski jump.

Lyngseidet seemed a lush place with its fine houses on the fringe of hayfields and wooded knolls. Hard to believe we were near the 70th parallel, in the same latitude as bits of Alaska, Greenland, and north Siberia. People spoke with dread of the cold of winter, even though the coast is under the influence of the Gulf Stream. Without it, this rich countryside would be frozen and barren as other places on the parallel.

D

Luck was with us here.   As we debated on the problem
of getting still farther north, two buses drew up, disgorging
some passengers, but leaving a sufficient number within to
indicate that the vehicles had not completed their journey.
We lost no time in contacting an English speaker and mentioned our difficulty.   The buses were going north to the
end of the road and we could get a lift if we were prepared
to crush in.   It was a crush, but we were greeted with
smiles.

It was a party of Finnish naturalists, botanists mostly,
with no less than two professors in their midst.   The limit
of the road was the northerly extremity of a tour which
had taken them through the tundra of Finland and Sweden
to Arctic Norway.

Their destination was the school-house at Fastdal.   The
speed at which they leapt into action there was an educa-
tion.   Tents and marquees were thrown on to the green
playground, and in no time mallets were thumping and
a village of canvas rising.

We camped down by the fjord, on a fine spot where a
glacial river discharged into the sea.   Beyond the tent flaps,
stretching across the mouth of the fjord, was a snowy island
—for all the world like our own Arran.   To the east were
snow-streaked hills as lumpy as the Cairngorms.   On the
west were the peaks we hoped to climb, cloud-capped, but
unmistakably Alpine.   Lying in our sleeping-bags at midnight looking out through the open door, we could see the
blurred disc of the sun shining through rain discharging
in veils from heavy clouds.

The familiar patter on the tent did not encourage early
rising, but by mid-day we were off, taking with us three
days' supply of food, sleeping-bags, and a large groundsheet
to make a bivouac.   Stupidly, we left the base camp standing.   A visit to a croft to buy a couple of loaves and we
headed up through the birches of a fine glen called the
Fastdalselv.

There was a path of sorts to begin with, leading through

peat stacks, and climbing by a sparkling torrent draining from a range of sharp rock peaks called the Fastdalstind. On the north side was a great scree ridge scattering its boulders almost at our feet. It made us feel tired to even think of toiling up that slope.

Where the streams split we took the north branch called the Kopangselv. Ahead of us was a glen becoming bare of vegetation where a tongue of stones and moraine descended from a bulging ice fall. With gladness we recognized a twin-peak we had seen from Jaeggevarre. It rose in 3,000 feet of rock from the west edge of the ice. We decided we would do a wall climb on it, rather than attack it by a mere ridge.

A convenient place having been selected for the bivouac, we had a meal, took a sandwich, and set off. The air was sultry and clouds brushed the tops of the peaks. The edge of the ice fall ended in a ravine below our feet. We were separated from our mountain by no mean obstacle, but apart from the detour involved, the lower part of the route was spouting with waterfalls whose sheerness indicated rock at an excessively high angle. Considerable reconnaissance would be necessary to find a route on this crag.

Instead, we made up the moraine to join the ice fall on its north-easterly edge. It looked difficult, being steep and riven with pinnacles and crevasses. The wall enclosing us was uncomfortably steep and rocky, the kind of place where you expect stones to fall, but we could detect no signs of recent falls, so considered it safe. The snow was loose on the surface, forcing us to test each snow-bridge thoroughly before trusting ourselves on the crevasses. Fifteen hundred feet of interesting work and we entered a basin from which a ring of sharp peaks rose in the rock ridges we remembered. Each had its own little hanging glacier. Fired by this sight, we made plans for climbing not one, but the whole lot. We thought we could do it in one go, so we were still pretty innocent.

Meantime we went for the highest peak, which threw

a rib down like the Observatory Ridge of Ben Nevis, but considerably steeper.   We should have gone for this instead of taking a safety-first line by a snow couloir abutting against the upper wall of the mountain.   It was excessively steep and contained a couple of *schrunds* which we were able to jump.   We kicked steadily upward on an unconsolidated surface, trying to banish from thought the consequences of an avalanche in this place.

We took turns at kicking, each change of lead bringing a little bay of rocks a thousand feet above closer and closer, till at last we could step on to it and the tension was relieved.   To our joy the rock was gabbro, sound as the stuff on Jaeggevarre, and Scott led up the first vertical pitch.   Above that the angle eased and we climbed swiftly in combination to a narrow notch under the topmost part of the mountain.

There was a cry of astonishment, and another, and another, as we assembled there, delighted.   Below us was the red ball of the sun, shedding its light on a fiery sea. Standing out of the loneliness of the Arctic Ocean were the dark shapes of islands, enchanting silhouettes.   The time was exactly midnight and a band of fire touched the snow cornice at our feet where it overhung a sheer sweep of cliffs.   Such magic does not occur very often in life. We sat on the summit of the Store Jaegervandstind until cold drove us along the south-west ridge.

From the upper glacier basin we had noted that this south-west ridge connected to a col a thousand feet down, rising again in a jagged edge of pinnacles to an exciting point of rock.   We had been intrigued by one particular part of that ridge, where a great bite had been taken out, leaving vertical walls like a gigantic edition of the Tearlach Dubh Gap. *   Any traverse of that ridge, we felt, would give superlative mountaineering.

It did too.   We climbed over ribbons of snow clinging to knife-edges of rock, and broad slabs overhanging space.

* A problem on the Cuillin Ridge of Skye.

Once or twice we thought we were at the notch, but there was no mistaking the true cleft when, dramatically, it was at our feet. The rocks literally beetled, preventing us from seeing into the floor of the gap ; and the wall on the far side appeared quite unclimbable. By way of challenge there was a tiny cairn of stones placed each side of the gap telling us that someone had crossed it. Twenty feet down we could see a rusted ring spike projecting from a crack, showing that mechanical aids had been used.

I proceeded to prospect, but was compelled to return to remove my sack and get rid of my ice axe ; the wall was too steep to allow of any encumbrances. The question was, if we got down, could we get up the other side ? If not, was there a possibility of return ? Scott went down empty-handed, protected by the rope, moving neatly out of sight, but taking such a time that I knew the climbing must be extremely difficult.

A shout that he was down, and he started up the other side. Climbing with infinite caution he moved into sight, literally a fly on a wall. He had reached a crack running leftwards which appeared to slant upwards over the main sweep of the exposed mountainside. Not a place for a nervous man.

He moved up the crack, then paused awhile. A few unsuccessful moves and then we saw him reach down with his right hand as though to tie a shoe-lace. He stooped to a position that looked as if he must inevitably fall. His right hand and right foot pulled him in to the wall where his face was squeezed hard against the rock. His disengaged left arm and left leg moved slowly forward, feeling for holds. The move was a pure balance ; it was the kind of place where " a well-directed push with a straw would have sent him to eternity ". Slowly we watched his left hand take a hold and his body straighten up as his point of balance was restored.

Such a move on an exposed wall calls for enterprise,

for the climber who makes it must be prepared to unmake it.   Fortunately Scott was not called upon to retrace his steps.   The climbing above was on good holds, and we soon heard his triumphant shout as he reached a ledge and found a good belay.   Our 120 feet of nylon rope was stretched across the gap reaching up to Scott's platform high above us.

We had 40 feet of spare rope, and the best way of using this length seemed for Watson to climb down into the gap safeguarded from above by me.   The kit could then be sent across the gap to Scott who would pull it up.   I would then climb down and tie on to the rope in the gap.

First of all I got Watson to leave a rope sling on the ring spike on his way down, so that I could get a thread belay for the first part of the descent.   He did this.   On reaching the sling I then doubled the rope through the sling so that I could slide down it for twenty feet. Unfortunately the most difficult part of the wall was un-suited to these manœuvres and I had to climb down under my own steam, unroped.   Both sides of that gap are severe by any standard.

Nothing could stop us now.   Climbing along an airy crest we traversed the flank of some pinnacles and found ourselves under the final tower—a finger of rock, steep as a building.   There may have been a frontal route on its smooth edge, but we were not looking for gymnastics of the super-severe sort.   Our eyes were fastened on a crack grooved out of the south wall where it sliced away in a thousand feet of red rock slabs.   The ledge ended under a pronounced overhang.

No finish to a climb could have been more delightful. The overhang was no more than a test of nerve, for the holds were jug-handles and ideally placed.   One could hang out and savour the tremendous drop below.   We literally pulled ourselves on to the top, the ideal way to finish a climb.

During the climb we had watched the peaks around us

change from the rose tint of Alpen-glow to pale gold. Far
away, we could now see the phenomenon being repeated
as the southern peaks caught their first rays of sunlight.
Even at this great distance we could see the vivid pink
suffusion changing to gold. Spasms of mist were spreading
over the northern ridges, enveloping the tops, then breaking in a whirl of vapour to reveal demon shapes of trolls
and jotuns. Our peak was appropriately named the
Trolltind.

Most Arctic in character was the westward view. Below
the plunge of gabbro walls was a lake, inky black by the
pearly Ulfsfjord, the Jaegervand or " Hunter's Lake ".
Land, desolate as a peat bog, enclosed it, a river of rubble
reaching from the mountain to it, showing that the glacier
must have cast its ice into these dark waters at one time.

On this grim shore we were astonished to see settlement
after settlement, like strung-out boulders each side of the
Jaegervand. However bleak it may be, it certainly was
not lonely. Across the Ulfsfjord was a country of com-
plete contrast. The sun shone on a rock strata that gleamed
with the brightness of limestone, and trees and little plots
of cultivation lighted the brown hills. We were to revise
our ideas on Jaegervand when we saw it free of shadow
in the sparkle of sunlight. It was from camps on this
shore that Mrs. Main, Hastings, Slingsby, etc. did their
pioneer work on the encircling peaks.

Sitting up here, enjoying the early hours of this still
morning, we had ample time to study Jaeggevarre. It
presented from this northerly aspect a sheer face of rock
crowned by rolling snow domes, its icy shoulders standing
high above everything else. Now that we could see its
long summit spread before us we realized just how much
ground we had covered in our twenty-three-hour climb
from the fjord.

With thoughts of climbing yet another mountain we
descended the south ridge, but long halts for photography
caused a kind of apathy to creep into our movements,

and a ring round the sun was taken to mean that a change of weather was brewing. It was.

From the col from which we would have climbed our peak we plunged down steep snow slopes, smooth except for one great crevasse. Jumping this, we were soon dashing down the glacier to be stopped short at the ice fall. In the twelve hours since the ascent our steps had melted, so we had to rekick the whole way down. It was after 9 a.m. when we got to the bivouac, and the first spots of rain were falling from an overcast sky.

No one suggested going down to base. All of us were keen on another peak, and anyhow, we had a large groundsheet. So, folding it over us like an envelope we tried to sleep. I felt very wide awake and just lay, being bitten by mosquitoes occasionally and feeling my sleeping-bag from time to time to see how wet it was getting.

The next thing I knew was Adam shaking me to wakefulness. Rain was drumming down and the upper part of my sleeping-bag was soaking since I was the outside man. " Come on, we'll need to clear out," he said. He reckoned without Scott. Douglas is one of those sensible men who sleep submerged inside the sleeping-bag, so that he never knows what goes on outside. The world was a pretty dismal place to him surfacing from its dark interior to the blinding reality of another day. His bleary eyes and hung head comprehended only one thing when we wakened him, sleep. And he told us in no uncertain terms that it was only a sanguinary shower that would pass. His relapse into deep breathing was the end of that argument. We edged under the groundsheet once more.

The next awakening was rude. A blast of wind whipped the sheet from us, the bonus of a shower-bath being deferred for just as long as it took us to crawl out of our bags. Clutching our gear, we made for some boulders and folded the sheet over us like a tent, our heads acting as poles, our posteriors as pegs. Inside this igloo we got the primus going for a fry of eggs and bacon, while the wind and rain battered outside.   As we were getting wet fast, and would be wetter before long, we lost no time in heading down.

Scrambling over slippery boulders, fording streams, stumbling through birches, we beat through the rain to the fjord.   Water splashed out of us.   The blessings of dry clothes and a big tent would not be long delayed now. We had a shock coming.   The tent had been blown down and dragged along the ground, leaving our stuff exposed to the rain.   Luckily, Scott had wrapped his gear in a waterproof cape.   Everything of mine, including dry clothes and photographic films, was sodden.

Bundling it up, and dumping what we could not carry, we made for a house nearby.   They understood our plight without question and soon we were treated to a fire and a share of their room.   Wearing my wet sleeping-bag as a kilt, my only dry garment one of Scott's pullovers, I stood as near the stove as possible, obscured by a pile of wet clothes steaming merrily.   Scott and Watson were in a rather better state.   Not until 10 p.m. did we manage to get a meal inside us.   The storm was still going strong when we bedded down on the floor.

Morning brought a wonderful transformation—the fjord flat calm, a warm sun, and a vivid brilliance in the landscape.   We repaired the great rips in the tent, got the clothing strung out to dry, and celebrated deliverance by a dumpling of Himalayan proportions and a baking of pancakes.

That evening we walked up the road to get a closer look at the Kopang glacier which, according to the Finnish professors, reached the sea within recent geological time.   The road was busy with villagers who hardly acknowledged our salutations.   Like the people from lower down the fjord they were mostly small and rather squat, without the dignified presence of the average Norwegian.   But they were probably shy, rather than uncouth.

When we did chat to one of them we were surprised at the ease with which we could follow his conversation.   He

spoke almost broad Scots at times, and his Norwegian was
delivered so slowly that we had time to interpret the full
sense of what he was saying.   It is the only occasion when
I have felt myself *au fait* with a foreign tongue.

At midnight we settled down, confident in the weather.
Over Arno island the sky was red-gold from the hidden
ball of the sun.   Soon it would appear in sight.   We lay
awhile waiting for it, then fell asleep.   I awoke to a furious
flapping of tent fabric and found the pegs had been up-
rooted and the poles tilted to the point of collapse.   Sorting
this, I fell asleep again to be wakened as the tent collapsed.
It was a case of " Action Stations ", and it was quite a
fight to hold the tearing canvas as Scott and Watson
removed the flysheet and weighted the pegs with stones.

In the grey of the morning we rose and caught a bus
to Lyngseidet.   To our disgust we arrived there too late
by one hour to catch the Tromso bus.   There was no other
until the following day.

We were diverted by our first close-up of Lapp women,
dressed like minstrels and pushing bicycles.   From the
handlebars dangled great bunches of fish.   The Lapps were
very small, with the brazen look of tinkers.   We were
rather repulsed by their sly faces.   A fish boat was being
unloaded and they shuttled back and fore with fish.

Slingsby mentions in his book (*Norway, The Northern
Playground*) that in his day there was a Lapp encampment
in the narrow neck of land between Kjosen Fjord in the
West and Lyngen Fjord in the east.   It is still thriving—
except that nowadays they have Nissen huts as well as
tents.   These people were from that camp.   We visited
the place later, and were glad to get away from it.

A Lapp in fancy dress of red tassels, brightly coloured
jerkin, knee-breeches, with a belt hung with an ornamental
knife at his waist, sat outside the first tent of reindeer
skins.   We could glimpse a bright fire burning inside, the
smoke forcing its way out through a hole in the roof.
Various dogs lay around, some weighted down with large

blocks of wood dangling from their necks. The gentleman in fancy dress gave a signal and a stout dame, presumably his wife, intercepted us to promote some trade. Boxes of fancy goods were presented to us. We bought some excellent gloves of soft wool at a reasonable price. Most of the other items were trifles made from reindeer horns.

Farther up the camp one of the women asked for money because I took her photo. She knew the English word for it too: the " Lapp of luxury ". Being a show-piece like this has a debasing effect. While we were there a large car drew up and a couple of American women got going with a ciné-camera. A noticeable bustle took place in the encampment as the best finery was hastily donned for acting the part.

We learned that a few weeks before, prosperity had descended on them when the American tourists from the *Caronia*, which had docked in the fjord, debouched hosts of wealthy passengers anxious to photograph these strange people and take samples of their art back to the U.S.A. An express lorry service to Tromso was at once flung into operation, bringing northward a cargo of polar bear skins, ermine pelts, Arctic fox furs, etc. So the hard streak of commercialism goes pretty far north.

By late afternoon we were considering a camp spot for a snooze when we had a stroke of luck, for we met the climbers from Lyngen school-house in full strength, like some strange assembly of trolls with their scraggy beards and baggy windproofs. To see new faces and hear new ideas was refreshing as a bath. Our difficulties were solved. There was a boat to Tromso due to sail at 2 a.m. from the head of Kjosen Fjord, and we would have company, for a party of them were catching it to make a landing and explore the Jaegervand region.

Meantime we were invited along to their schoolhouse and have a meal. We even had a tune on Falconer's recorder, between hearing of their many fine climbs and cross-country expeditions in the two months since arriving here.

They told us how all this had come about. For eighteen months they had been planning to come here, primarily to climb, and train themselves for bigger things, to build up experience, and do such scientific work as the composition of the party allowed. Love of mountains was the activating force, and for some members of the party it meant a considerable sacrifice of income, for none were men of leisure. They had always wanted to go on an expedition, and had taken the correct course of action by not waiting to be invited on someone else's party, but had organized an expedition themselves. All were members of a club called the Oread Mountaineering Club, a group formed in the Midlands three years before with the idea of spreading the gospel of simplicity in mountain approach.

How well they did their work can be gauged from the fact that over forty peaks were climbed, many by new routes, and four of them for the first time. In addition, their geographical, geological, and glaciological work will be an invaluable aid to future travellers in this scarcely-known terrain.

It is particularly gratifying that in 1952 their leader, George Sutton, led another group to Spitzbergen on a sledging trip. They have plans for the Himalayas in 1955.

Talking of mountains we forgot the rain as we walked to Kjosen Fjord to catch the boat at 2 a.m.

CHAPTER VI

Of Sea Journeys and Matters Incidental

IT was as grey as a wet day in Glasgow, and the rain was just as heavy, when blasts on a siren announced the arrival of the boat. It was a neat little craft, a " Victory " ship with an empty first-class lounge, and as there was no one to say us nay, we promptly stretched ourselves at full length in the sleeping-bags. Astonishingly, we were allowed to lie undisturbed till breakfast time, so our memories of this ship shine brighter than the dismal dawn patrols associated with other voyages.

Where the boat went during this blissful sleep I have no idea, but the Jaegervand peaks were to starboard when we went on deck, glacier snouts and snowfields gleaming, and craggy ridges spouting upward into clouds fluffy as cotton wool. It was our first distant view of them as a mountain range, unobscured by intervening ridges. The clouds were breaking, and with excitement we watched spike after spike thrusting through—a gigantic Cuillin of Skye with the Store Jaegervandstind occupying the position of Sgurr Alasdair, and the Trolltind, which had given us our " Tearlach Dubh Gap ", sticking up like a gigantic molar tooth above the knife-edge of its ridge.

The houses strung along this shore were close at hand ; the same that we had seen from the tops, looking like boulders on the edge of desolation. What had looked like a bleak moor was revealed as green, wooded peninsula, the houses brightly colourful on their squares of crofting land by the clear Ulfsfjord.   The anchorage of Jaegervand with its river rising to the " Hunter's Lake " is the perfect place for exploring this group, and Mrs. Main* knew what she was about when she chose it.

At a point on the Northern peninsula we said our good-byes to the four Oread boys, who transferred themselves to a little boat sent out from the shore to collect passengers and cargo.   The Lyngen peaks disappeared to leeward as we headed west on a glass-like ocean on which flocks of guillemots and razorbills bobbed and dived.   Puffins passed to and fro, still in the red-nosed stage.   Gathering passengers steadily at quaint little places in the Grotsund, we reached Tromso at 2 p.m., as clouds borne on a cold southerly wind filled the sky.

Tromso is what I would call a real old-fashioned town, the kind of place a reader of Arctic books might expect, a place of wooden walls, narrow streets, and a harbour full of ships, from Arctic whalers and Grimsby trawlers, to coal boats from Spitzbergen. Many shops had furs for sale, sealskins, polar bear, ermine (30 shillings each), mink (£50 for four), Arctic fox, and many others.   Scott wanted a suitable pelt for his kilt sporran, but no known animal had a fur priced low enough to suit his pocket.   His unkempt figure handling these magnificent skins, suitable for Duchesses and Dowagers, was indeed an incongruous sight.

Having seen the town we tried to get into the museum, but it had not yet got over its disruption due to the war, so there was nothing for it but try the library, for our boat to Lofoten was not due to sail until 1.30 a.m.   Here we were received with welcome, the girls raking the shelves for books on birds and sitting down beside us to interpret the language.

In Norway they have the excellent custom of opening

* See *Mountaineering in the Land of the Midnight Sun* for Mrs. Main's pioneering exploits in this region.

the cinemas during the day so that tickets may be booked for either of the two evening performances. We had booked for the British feature, *The Queen of Spades*, a celluloid version of the Pushkin short story, and it was amusing to hear the reaction of an unsophisticated audience to this tale. There were gasps and murmurs from time to time, becoming a cry of horror when the camera suddenly pin-pointed the dead face of the ancient Countess in her coffin. The producer would have been proud at the success of his efforts could he have heard that piece of audience reaction. Not since my penny matinee days have I enjoyed such uninhibited entertainment.

The harbour at midnight was gloomy with rain and the dimness of dusk. Boats were lit up and fog-horns sounded as ships went and ships came, big cargo ships and little fishing vessels.

A little man, broad-shouldered and powerful-looking, came over for a chat. Eyeing our ice axes he asked if we had been in Spitzbergen. He had skippered the first Oxford Spitzbergen Expedition in 1921 and remembered Seton Gordon with his bagpipes, and hides for watching birds. George Binney, too, he remembered, and Julian Huxley, but try as he would he could not recall Dr. Tom Longstaff, who was also in that distinguished party. The skipper's name was Leif Jensen and he was now on a shore job in the cargo shed.

There was no cover aboard the boat when it did come in, but there were a couple of partially protected life-belt boxes like broad coffins, and with the groundsheet folded on top of them we were at least clear of the wet deck. Inside sleeping-bags we forgot the drizzle so successfully that it was mid-day before we crawled out. A kindly seaman had washed round us at 5 a.m., leaving us un-disturbed. Slingsby's Stedtind lay off the port bow, clean as a pebble and as bare. We felt rather ashamed to be creeping past this peak for the second time and doing nothing about it.

But Lofoten was calling, and over there the sun was shining. By mid-afternoon we had turned the Raftsund corner under the green island of Store Molla. The rock skerries dotting the Oyhelle Sund shone red on the sea, and high above, snow cornices glistened like some celestial washing on a line. Between was a succession of rock ridges and curving buttresses, beckoning us to waste no time in getting there.

But first of all we had to go to Svolvær and stoke up with food for our forthcoming campaign. A night in our old quarters and we could catch the boat next day. We felt we had never been away when we looked out next day to the familiar sight of rain sweeping across the misty mountains and leaden clouds hanging over the town. The difference this time was that we got shelter in the fo'c'sle of the milk boat instead of being half-perished on deck.

The " Goat " was quite a sight as we pulled out of Svolvær. It was a shadow, narrow as a pencil, veiled by a gauze of thin mist of intangible height. The " horns " sprouted unbelievably out of space, seeming to nod to us. As our barometer of weather we interpreted this affability as a sign that the weather gods might spare us a smile.

This time we were heading for Rulten—said to be the finest of all Lofoten peaks, with climbing as fine as the best of the Chamonix Aiguilles. We were expecting to be welcomed with open arms here, for there is a croft with the name of Reknes at the foot of Rulten, and in it we hoped to find a very charming girl called Esther Kristoffersen. Earlier in the year Esther had been in Scotland, and we had the pleasure of ski-ing with her on the Scottish hills. By reports, she was now back home and we were going to give her a surprise.

Some sharp blasts on the hooter and a little boat pulled out from the shore in answer to our greeting. If Esther's brother knew who we were he made no sign, but loaded our camping kit in the stern and whisked us in powerful strokes to a little shed. She was there waiting for us—

5. Head of the Kjosen Fjord in the Lyngen peninsula.   From here we sailed to Tromso
(Chapter V)

36. The mountains of Lyngen from the west. In the centre is the Store Jaegervands
tind and the Trolltind, stretching from the prominent glacier on the left to the bank
of low cloud on the right. The average height of this range is around 5,000 feet
(*Chapter V*)

37. One of the little whaling boats that fish the Vest Fjord. A carcase is slung amid-
ships, the jaws hanging downwards (*Chapter V*)

58. Lyngen peninsula from the west, showing the forested lower slopes and great slopes of weathered gabbro (*Chapter V*)

59. The croft of Reknes in the Oyhelle Sund, near which we based our camp for the ascent of the peaks seen in this photograph (*Chapter VI*)

40. (*left*) The house where we received so much hospitality. The carpets are home-spun, and most of the furniture is home-made. The fish-pot simmers on the peat-burning stove. Esther keeps her niece company by the fireside while her fisherman brother reads a magazine (*Chapter VI*)

41. (*below*) The family at Reknes—fine, warm-hearted people. Clara the carpet weaver is on the left, and her two children are in the front row (*Chapter VI*)

42. Our camp at Reknes, surrounded by great rock slabs (*Chapter VII*)

43. Towering over Reknes is the peak of Rulten, clear at last, with every crag and snow patch reflected in the green waters of the Oyhelle Sund. We climbed the peak by its left-hand edge, the final pinnacle being surmounted by the right edge, above the tiny snow patch shown in the photo (*Chapter VII*)

44. A mere spur of Rulten, rising in one surge of granite slabs from the sea. The
real climb on Rulten started from beneath the left wall of this pinnacle (*Chapter VII*)

45. (*left*) Lofoten walls. A character-istic of the Lofotens are these tremendous slabs of unweathered granite, offering little hand- and foothold to the climber, and often supporting a rich flora of moss and Alpine flowers. These were the reputedly un-climbable peaks
(*Chapter VII*)

46. (*below*) Looking south-eastward from a rock spur on Rulten to Store Molla (*left*) and Little Molla (*right*). Beyond the islands is the open Vest Fjord, the whole area providing the richest cod-fishing in Norway (*Chapter VII*)

Rulten could sulk in the clouds as long as it liked. With cups of coffee and cakes in our hands we heard the latest from Glasgow and Lofoten, for Esther talks with skill in both tongues. Her Scottish accent was further improved before we left.

Our immediate concern was a camp spot, and though we were invited to use the barn, we preferred to camp if the ground was suitable. The hayfield seemed to be a crop of flowers, of purple vetch, dwarf cornel, bladder campion, golden potentillas, St. John's wort, cranesbill, etc. We pitched the tent near a row of brown peat stacks, the lightest coloured peat I had ever seen.

Below us the shore curved in two little bays enclosing the narrow headland of Reknes. Glimpses of black slabs and fearsome mountain walls kept us on the alert for a clearing. It came with a blast of wind that sent the mist spinning. Great fingers of rock appeared three thousand feet above us, their naked buttresses plunging down to polished slabs disappearing into the sea. Glacier ice and snow gullies rent these fastnesses of pinnacle and shattered ridge. We had never seen anything to compare with this for verticality. Visibility closed down immediately and a storm of wind and rain set in.

After sixteen hours it was still hard at it. The tent had held magnificently and we had given up taking alarm. All round us the ground was sodden, under water in places, but inside we were merely damp. As a relief from reading, cooking, and writing, we thought it time we paid a further visit to the house.

They thought our visit long overdue. All were busy in the making of a carpet. Inside the workshop was a treadle loom worked by Esther's sister Clara. Everyone had a job to do. Clara's little girls cut up discarded clothing into long strips and sewed them together to wind on to a bobbin as a continuous strip of various colours. The grannie operated a revolving frame on which thick thread—the base material of the carpet—was speedily wound. Clara

E

at the loom worked swiftly, inserting the bobbin back and fore through the thread, each clamp of the treadle adding an inch or so of carpet.

I was curious about this spinning business. I had watched it closely in the Himalayas, where it is done by moving a complicated arrangement of sticks up and down, the result being the transformation from wool to clothing. Here was the same kind of arrangement, mechanized up to a point it is true, but basically the same. I was determined to get to the bottom of it.

Clara explained it. A good spinner could make thirty feet of carpet in a day, provided there was a sufficiency of old clothing. So saying, her eyes alighted on my climbing breeches—old friends with the rips and darns of many a campaign. I did not need to know Norwegian to interpret that look. She had them from me too, and exhibited them to me a few days later as a strip of warm brown carpet. Every time she wipes her feet she will think of me, she said.

We saw examples of really fine work in the best room, not only in carpets, embroidery, and lace, but in woodwork of superb craftsmanship, tea-trays, ashtrays, and decorative work made by Esther's brothers. While the women had been spinning the two boys had been making fishing nets, working at terrific speed from string on a wooden spool. Life in such a place as this calls for an all-round knowledge of so many things, from the baking of bread and equipping a home, to the vast skills of land and sea.

We asked Esther how she liked being back home. She found it quiet, too quiet. Her town life had unsettled her, and she talked of going to Oslo to be a nurse. We did our best to persuade her that life here was worth more than the superficial attractions of the town, even if she had to put on her wellington boots and climb five hundred feet in the rain to bring in the cows, in the middle of our sales talk. I am glad to say we won her over, and she is now training to be a nurse in Lofoten.

Having the free run of the place we learned much of what life in Lofoten means to families dependent on a small boat and a patch of stony land on the fringe of the mountains.   As in other parts of Norway, the solid founda- tion of their lives is the large family unit.   To gather the harvest of the fields and the sea needs sons and daughters, and a happy social life inside and outside the family is the result.   (In a dance which began on an adjacent island at midnight, the last boats left for home at 7 a.m.)

The main jobs of the farm are the cutting of peats in May and June for the long Arctic winter, the planting of vegetables, and harvesting the hay.   Getting in the hay crop is the most important job of summer, for the number of cattle and sheep that can be kept through the winter depends upon it.   This is a real family affair, with the menfolk swinging their scythes on the hillsides, and women and children hanging the mown grass on long drying frames like fences, specially erected for the purpose.   Given three days of good weather it is then ready for manhauling in nets to the barn, a strenuous job in terrain where horses cannot be used.   The method might well be tried in the West Highlands.

But it is fishing that puts money in their pockets.   A good fisherman fishes eleven months out of any twelve— following the cod in spring from Lofoten to Finnmark, or changing over in midsummer to whaling.   In this latitude, each summer brings a migration of small whales to the Vest Fjord area.   Though technically " small ", these whales are far from small when you see a carcase slung across the deck for flensing.   The normal fishing craft is used, except that a " crow's nest " is tied to the mast and a harpoon gun mounted on the bow.

By the end of summer or late autumn, the herring shoals should be pushing their way through the water, providing good fishing until the arrival of King Cod announces another Lofoten season.   No fishing bank in the world can compare with the Vest Fjord at this time, when in the short space of six weeks over 160,000 tons of fish may be caught.

The boats engaged are a joy to the eye, from the graceful point of the Viking prow to the beautifully rounded stern. If Lofoten has a song it is the " thump-thump " of their engines, beating up and down the narrow sounds, twisting between rock skerries, or slipping to anchorage as neatly as rowing boats.

Along the whole 1,200 miles of Norwegian coast-line, you will see these little craft—spruce and well painted, most of them products of the post-war world, for much of the Norwegian fleet was destroyed in the war. The present vitality of the fishing industry is due as much to imaginative planning ashore as hard fishing at sea. Fishermen know that what they bring from the water will finish up as food or factory produce. Modern fishing schools and radar make fishing more than a merely manual craft.

The cod arrive in Lofoten waters in jostling shoals one hundred and fifty feet thick. They are followed by hawkers, pedlars, jugglers, tricksters, etc., who hope to reap their share of the harvest from the thronging fishermen.

There is nothing haphazard about the fishing. To keep the peace, fishing grounds are numbered, and areas are allotted to each craft. Echo-sounding craft give locations and depth of the cod shoals each morning before the boats leave at 8 a.m. They must return by 8 p.m. Gill nets, set before coming in, are taken up in the morning. Other boats use long lines with over a thousand hooks.

No strong drink is allowed on board any boat, although the height of the cod fishing season in Arctic waters of the same latitude as north Alaska and central Greenland is the coldest time of year. This regulation is rigidly enforced by Government patrol boats, and having seen some Norwegians in their cups, I do not question the wisdom of it. The Gulf Stream flowing north between Iceland and Britain keeps the fishing ports ice-free at all times.

Talking of these things, and plied with coffee from time to time, we gradually reached the singing stage. Esther and her mother played the guitar in soft accompaniment to lilting folk tunes and hill-billies of the Western trails. Our contribution was a brace of bothy ballads of North-East Scotland—a raucous rendering delivered with more energy than melody. Then we were shown the treasures of the fishing shed, with its floats, nets, hooks, masts, tools, etc.

After three days of rain, during which time we fished, dried our clothes, and shifted our camp to a less sodden piece of ground, there came a morning when we awoke to birds calling and skies flecked with blue. All forenoon the clouds streamed off the peaks till at last they were clear, every crag and snow patch reflected to perfection in the green waters of the sound. Magpies were chattering as if it was the first day of spring, and flocks of fieldfares and twites foraged in the fields.

To capture this in colour and monochrome was imperative so it was cameras alert and out in a boat for view-points. Esther trailed a fishing line astern and we hardly noticed the large catch she was hauling in.

Perhaps we should have climbed that afternoon, but I preferred to wait and give the rocks a chance to dry. Further, Magnar Pettersen had suggested that he would join us this very day and we did not want him to find us gone. As the weather had dulled there was no hardship in waiting. We went to bed when he failed to arrive.

Magnar wakened us at 7 a.m. He had been on the tops, having crossed over a ridge in the north and dropped three thousand feet to our camp. He reported a fine night with about two hours of sunshine before rain set in, driving him down to our tent.

Now he was going off on a long row. A boat he had borrowed for the climb would need to be returned, and he was separated from it by four miles of water.

So he would require another boat which in turn would need to be returned. Cheerfully he waved us goodbye and we turned our attention to Rulten. It was now or never.

CHAPTER VII

Rulten

MAGNAR had simplified the mountain for us by advising us to go for the east ridge. He gave no details, but merely said we should find much " air " below our boots, and that sounded good enough for us. The sun was now full blaze and our hearts were high as we struck along the coast, heading for a little col where a triple-pointed spur of Rulten dropped to a gap before rising in one mighty sweep of rock to the ultimate point of the mountain.

Our delight at being on the move was somewhat miti-gated by a dense forest of ferns and birches that clung to the steep hillside between us and the rock haven above. Sweating profusely, we slipped on boulders and clung to birches till at last we were on hard snow and could walk easily to the col. We had gained five hundred feet per-haps, and the view over the other side was dramatic.

A rock wall dropped from the triple peak in one terrific plate of granite, too steep and smooth for any mortal man. It ended in a green glen sparkling with waterfalls leaping in a final fling into the bay at our feet. Beyond that was the Vest Fjord, glittering like silver in *contre-jour* light, the great hulks of its islands mysterious and lonely, bearing a timeless quality. Emphasizing the stillness was the " thump-thump " of a fishing boat, the only one on the water this Sabbath day.

This was a place for photography. We were high enough to get a feeling of both depth and height into our

pictures, and we " shot " north, south, and east, from the
ravine of the Raftsund to the bright emerald of a glacier
lake at our feet.

The climbing started at once from this point, with an
overhanging corner. A shoulder from Scott and I was
soon up it, and engaged on a typically granite pitch. The
rock was like flint underfoot, and progress could only be
made where its smooth slabs were jointed or cleft by cracks
and chimneys. It was strenuous, pushing-and-pulling
climbing, not the delicate balance type, with much moss
and dirt filling these lines of weakness.

Clouds obscured the sun, and the sky was taking its old
familiar leaden hue before we reached the first pinnacle
a thousand feet above. Scott had been finding the climbing difficult in nails, and at this point, threat of rain or
no, he discarded his boots for plimsolls. His blood was
up and he took over the lead.

We were now separated from the main mountain wall
by a conspicuous rock tower several hundreds of feet high.
It proved difficult, and dirty, but gave stimulating climbing. An easier line could have been found, but Scott went
straight ahead, forcing chimneys, slabs, cracks, wedging up
minor overhangs, and straddling detached blocks to its top.

Another rock tower lay ahead, not so big or so formidable
as the preceding one, but the view from its top made us
think. I deposited my ice axe here, knowing full well
that the face ahead would permit of no encumbrances.
Immediately below us the flank of our tower fell sheer for
four hundred feet. Across the gap rose a sweep of tapering
slabs bare as a city tenement, soaring to a narrow point
which was the top of the peak. " Well, if there is a route
there, I can't see it," said Scott.

This is what a writer in the *Fell and Rock Club Journal*
said when he saw this face from farther off : " There stood
the savage Rulten. . . . We gazed with awe at the many
hundreds of feet of perpendicular slabs which constitute
the top of this desperate mountain."

Few faces are perpendicular. Seen *en face* they have the illusion of perpendicularity. The first job was to get into the gap four hundred feet below us. Moving one at a time on this steep descent we had plenty of opportunity of studying the face. It was obvious that any direct attack would require to go up the right-hand edge.

We went to work on it straight away. It was not perpendicular, and we made height fast, climbing by chimney and slab to reach a small patch of snow visible in the photograph (Plate 43). We were near the top, we knew, and went to work with some determination at a narrow crack, quite vertical and holdless in its lower part. Hoisting up the leader he managed to jam an arm in it, and adhere long enough to reach something higher up. It was a hard move, with faith at a low ebb and friction almost nil from rubber shoes on wet rock.

Scott took his revenge at being urged up such a place when we came to an impasse two hundred feet higher up. We were now under the summit, but prevented from reaching it by a bulge of cliff with one improbable line of weakness, where a curving crack bit deeply into an overhang. He looked at this while I unroped and traversed to the north edge of the mountain to see if there was anything over the other side.

The sight was pretty shocking. I looked down a cliff that arched in one black plunge to the green of glacier ice one thousand five hundred feet down. A narrow ledge running out from where I stood gave access to a vertical recess about forty feet high, poised above the drop. The place looked climbable, and seemed to conform to Magnar's description of much " air " beneath the feet of the climber. I shouted my news to Scott and pointed out the route. " Right, on you go," he said.

Anchored on the ridge, they signalled that they were ready, and I moved along the wall out of their sight. I found myself facing a square-cut chimney, too broad to span with back and knees, but split with two parallel cracks a shoulder's-width apart. Progress could be made with a foot and hand jammed in each crack, but the holds were slippery and the climbing was strenuous. The final move was over a jammed stone blocking the exit in an overhang. In the preoccupation of hauling myself over I hardly noticed the sensational position of my boot-heels. Listening to the scuffling of my feet, but quite unable to see what was going on, had proved quite exciting to the others.

As the others climbed, I had ample time to reflect on the fate of anyone unlucky enough to " come-off " on this pitch. But the place was not more than " very difficult " by rock climbing standards, and therefore quite within the capabilities of most competent rock climbers. A rope-sling anchored to a block of rock showed that the route was indeed the one mentioned by Magnar.

The top was at hand and we perched by the cairn, trying to shelter from the rain that was now sweeping in gathering strength from the south. It spoiled our peace of mind, for instead of revelling in what we could see of a view, our minds were turned on what we knew would be a slow and slippery descent on soaking wet rock.

From this eyrie we seemed to be perched right above the Oyhelle Sund, looking over peaks and slashes of water to the square silhouette of the Stedtind—monstrous even at this distance. Around us was a forest of pinnacles, blurred and misshapen with rain. We made down.

We had no intention of climbing down the cleft. Slipping the rope through the anchored rope-sling, we tested it for strength, then slid down it to the lower ledge. Rope or rope-sling breaking was not to be thought of here. The climbing called for constant care, and route-finding was far from easy. The crack that had moved Scott to protests on the way up proved a teaser coming down, for there was no hitch for a doubled rope. Nor was the 400-foot ascent from the gap easy. Where the route could be safeguarded by rope-slings, these aids were used.

Concentrated on the climb, our senses screwed to the rocks immediately ahead, we suddenly became aware of a light below our feet, a shimmering band of fire. Lofoten wall was spanned by a rainbow that swept in a great arc over land and sea ; burning brighter every moment as searchlights of gold pierced the dark clouds, picking out a peak here and there till every boulder and crag was aglow with crimson. By contrast to this searching colour, the low land and sea were in spectacular gloom, impenetrably deep.

This glorious vision of splendour and beauty faded quickly, and, addressing ourselves once more to the task, we pressed down, finding the climbing easier as we sought the line of least resistance. Quite suddenly, we seemed to be on the col below the triple peak.

We should have known to expect nothing but steep slopes of evilly disposed boulders, camouflaged with ferns and dwarf birch. In our innocence we thought we could detect a line avoiding all this, a grassy route which would lead to a small glacier lake situated above our camp. The falls and pitfalls between us and that glacier lake would make a sorry tale itself. Little did we expect a further Slough of Despond when we got there. The place where we expected good walking was a morass, so we had to take to the scrub once more, forcing a way over the last rise to find ourselves in camp. The climb had taken fifteen hours for a peak only 3,400 feet above the sea.

We should have slept well that night, but we did not. It had been cold on the mountain. At sea level it was muggy, a night for mosquitoes, and they were out in force. To lie in one's sleeping-bag was to be roasted, to lie out was to anticipate a thousand bites as these pests zoomed round one's ears.

*   *   *   *   *

Rulten was climbed for the first time in 1903 by J. N. Collie's party, which appropriately included W. C. Slingsby.

The route followed appears to have been left of the line we took, and by-passing the upper slabs by a traverse from the second last pinnacle across the face to the south ridge. This led easily to the summit. Collie says of it : " The climbing was good throughout, though nowhere of any great difficulty. Rulten is a fine rock peak. Its slabs and precipices may be said to start almost out of the sea. Any mountain that can give three thousand feet of bare rock, most of it set at an angle of over 70°, must be treated with respect." The climb was repeated in 1904 by some members of the same party.

Until 1938 there are only two other records, the route being roughly the same, but described as being difficult.

The peak has been climbed several times since, the route taken by us being the one followed by the local climbers from Svolvær who are very much disciples of the modern school. We thought the climb was of an overall high standard, exposed, and never excessively difficult, but always calling for sound mountaineering tactics.

CHAPTER VIII

Both Sides of Oyhelle Sund

WHEN Magnar visited our camp we had drawn his attention to three spiky peaks to the south of Rulten. Had they been climbed, we wondered? The seaward peak was particularly attractive, its simple architecture being one north-facing piece of stone sweeping from base to summit in a tapering slab, the smoothest we had ever seen. Its southern support was a flying buttress beginning as a bulge and shooting upwards in a parallel sweep for most of one thousand five hundred feet.

Access would be by the green glen sparkling with water-falls we had seen from Rulten (Plate 45). We had noted that this glen climbed swiftly to a bare corrie of boulders, becoming a deep shaded recess filled with old snow. From a col above, it looked possible to make an interesting ridge traverse of the three tops. Direct frontal attack on these seaward slabs seemed impossible.

Magnar knew of no ascent of these peaks. If we could borrow a boat this would be the ideal way of spending a day which promised to be fair. We had no wish to try another battle with the dense vegetation of the lower slopes.

There was no trouble about the boat, and we glided across the south bay, feeling that this effortless progress was the way to really enjoy mountains. We moored the boat where the stream emptied itself into the bay, wishing as we left it that we had better knowledge of the tides. The glen was as enchanting as it had seemed from

Rulten.   Flowers and emerald mosses decked its waterfalls, and its flanks provided walking so easy that we felt we were on a magic carpet.   Red rock slabs leapt on each side. The sea was behind, and the snow saddle hung ahead of us.

We rose swiftly to the col, but not in time to beat the clouds which were filling in from all directions.   On hard snow and scrambly rock we gained the first top to find a little moss-covered cairn planted on the highest point.

The second was more difficult, but without any obstacle capable of stopping a mountaineer, and as we had feared, this top also carried a cairn.   Our last hope was the seaward peak, which looked so sharp-pointed that we approached it buoyed with hope that we might still make a first ascent.

From a narrow col we faced a series of chimneys and grassy ledges leaping to a final block.   A couple of vertical cracks led to our third disappointment that morning.   A few mossy stones were perched on the topmost point.   I imagine these must have been planted by Professor Norman Collie's party in 1903 or 1904, for he would not neglect such a striking little mountain group.   We were prevented from looking over the slabs, unfortunately, by an unclimbable wall immediately below us.   But what we did see was not encouraging to a climber.

It was dull and grey as we retraced our steps to the snow corrie for a quick glissade and run down to the shore, where we had a shock.   The boat was high and dry, separated from the sea by 100 yards of boulders.   Hauling it was going to be hard work.   Pushing as the others pulled, I disappeared into a hole of water, to emerge gasping like a newly landed cod.

With much pulling and pushing we got the boat in the water and slung out fishing lines as we pulled northward. We fished with more intensity than usual, for tonight we needed fish for our supper, there was nothing else in the larder.   And the blighters would not rise.   Thoroughly soaked by my recent immersion I was dropped ashore while the others took over the trawl. They returned to camp triumphant with one large and one small cod and a fine saithe. As they sizzled in the pan a rising wind shook the tent canvas and the first blatter of rain drummed on the canvas. Our climb had been well timed.

On a prolonged mountaineering trip there comes a stage when one's clothing begins to become offensive, and it is then time to do a little washing. As it was still dull and rainy looking, and there was no time like the present, we commandeered washing boards and tubs from the croft and set to work. Shirts, shorts, underclothing, towels, socks, were duly washed, and in a fit of zeal I even scrubbed my Grenfell jacket till it shone whiter than its original colour.

With spotlessly clean hands we now took opportunity to have a baking of pancakes and hold a party in the tent, Esther being the guest of honour.

*   *   *   *   *

Wednesday, 8th August, dawned the finest morning we were to see in Norway. At 4 a.m. every mountain was clear, slabs and snowfields glistening with diamond light. The sound was still as a mill-pond, and magpies filled the air with their chattering. We had never realized the extraordinary vocabulary of this species until we heard their morning conversations outside the tent. There can be no doubt that they have a language full of meaning to each other.

This morning we intended to go north to the Store Trolltind and try to reach its summit, situated 3,428 feet above the fjord mentioned in Chapter III as being the wildest in Norway. To get there meant a four-mile row to our old camping spot at Korsnes.

Confronted by such a row, it is wise to praise the oarsman, and on this occasion neither Watson nor myself spared our praises as we lolled comfortably, dangling fishing hooks from prow and stern, while Scott plied in strong Cambridge

strokes. He was the only fish that rose to our bait.
Around each headland was a prospect of mountain and sea,
all of it familiar by now, but never seen to such perfection.
Bees hummed back and fore across the water on this still
morning.

There was a tent pitched on our old camping site at
Korsnes, and a boat was moored by the cove. We tied
up alongside and headed up under the peak of Trakta,
stopping now and then to fill our mouths with ripe bilberries.
We followed a bubbling stream that emptied itself in cascade after cascade from the rocky heart of the mountain.

We were in a horseshoe of red-grey slabs ragged as a
saw-blade where they reared against the sky. Snow hung
like aprons from hollows and long gullies. This is what
we had lost in a week's bad weather at Korsnes.

Our route to the biggest mountain " went " surprisingly
easily—up a stone shoot like Alasdair of Skye, then on
steep snow to a couloir on the south face. An overhanging
rock pitch blocked the way here. There was no direct
ascent of it, but we managed to turn it on the left by
descending a hundred feet and climbing a rock buttress
to a point where a traverse could be made to rejoin the
gully.

One more rock pitch and we heard a shout of welcome
from the top of the gully. It was the owner of the tent,
Lars Hansen, a local climber with a terrific reputation.
Lars had been on top of the peak and was now on his way
down. We were glad to hear we were not on the usual
route.

This col was a delightful spot, and we sat warm in the
sun. Above us was a fierce pinnacle like a spear called
Princessa. Lars had the honour of naming it, for he
pioneered the route up. So far, the climb has not been
repeated. These Norwegian climbers are most certainly
men of considerable enterprise, and when they classify
anything as severe or very severe, it is a judgement that
will suit a climber of any school. Princessa is very severe.

Looking northward from Reknes to the great rock peaks of the Raftsund. Trakta (*left*), Store Trolltind, Store Korsnestind and Little Korsnestind (*Chapter VIII*)

8. An unexpected meeting on a Lofoten mountain with Lars Hansen (*left*), a noted Nordland mountaineer. Adam Watson (*centre*), Douglas Scott (*right*) (*Chapter VIII*)

49. In the harvest field. Building up the cut hay on the drying frames for quick drying Note the peak stacks in the background, for burning during the long winter night (*Chapter VIII*)

50. The little glaciers of Lofoten which swell upward in concave snow-bulges smooth as silk, decorated here and there with patches of ice, green as bottle-glass. The summits are Getigaljartind and Higrafstind above the Trollfjord (*Chapter VIII*)

51. The house is of weatherboard with a turf roof. Looking southward to the Vest Fjord the hay can be seen drying on its long racks (*Chapter VIII*)

52. The northward view from the hayfield, looking to the Store Trolltind (left) and the Korsnestind. A profusion of flowers sprouts from the roof (*Chapter VIII*)

53. Haymaking beneath the low light of the midnight sun (*Chapter VIII*)

54. Lofoteners. Esther and Kirsty of Reknes with bilberries which they have been gathering on the hill (*Chapter VIII*)

55. The Trondheim Nid, a river busy with fishing craft and little boats of all kinds
(Chapter IX)

56. (*left*) Most of Trondheim is modern, the original town having been destroyed by various fires. These old warehouses are remnants of the original wooden town (*Chapter IX*)

57. This might be anywhere on the long north coast of Norway. It is the sea-front of Ålasund, where kittiwake gulls nest on the window ledges (*Chapter IX*)

With the invitation to join him in camp for a cup of coffee, Lars left us. We climbed by a great breast of snow to scramble over rocks that led us speedily upward in eight hundred feet to the summit.

Great changes had taken place in the month since we had last been in this part of the world. What had been unbroken ice and snow hemming the Trollfjordvand was now rent by summer rains and thaw. Icebergs floated on the green surface of the water three thousand feet below us. And the snow walls hemming its Coruisk-like setting had retreated to the fringe of the glaciers.

These glaciers rose steeply, swelling in concave snow bulges smooth as silk, decorated here and there with patches of ice, green as a glass bottle. Rock buttresses hemmed these north-western recesses, some of them offering challenging climbs, others hopelessly smooth and over-hung. These summits of Getigaljartind and Higrafstind are anything but minor peaks seen from this side. Worn into fantastic towers and pinnacles, the ridges soared with the grandeur and inaccessibility of an Alpine range. A lifetime of climbing could be spent in this tremendous basin.

Northward, we looked over a jumble of islands and peaks stretching from the strange lumpy tops of the " Blue Mountains "—the colour of their name—to the snow peak of Moisalen on the adjacent island of Hinnoy. Mountain tops stretched their rugged heads from the islands to the Mainland. Who has explored them all ? One would never have guessed from up here that there could be any exit to the sea from the gorge-like defile of the Trollfjord.

We descended the peak by the route taken by Lars, a fast run on snow taking us to a ridge of the Korsnestind where a little rock chimney led over to Brakset glen by a horrible slope of ferns and boulders. The old crofter who had supplied us with milk and eggs and lent us his boat, was busy with his hay when we suddenly appeared. His delight at seeing us again was quite touching.

F

Lars was seated outside his tent, a wireless set playing at his side as he pumped his primus stove. In such a wild setting it was incongruous to hear a metallic female voice singing " I've got you under my skin ".

That coffee was good, very good, and we pulled the boat with a will on the strength of it, Scott dangling the fishing line as Adam and I pulled the homeward miles. Whatever was wrong with the Oyhelle Sund this day I do not know, but we caught only two small fish in eight miles of rowing.

Lars had been keen on a difficult climb, and when we sailed away, it was agreed that we would return next day for an attempt on the twin peak of Trakta. This superb peak rising immediately behind his tent had figured largely in our speculations in the bad weather we had endured at its base. Lars knew a worthy route, and we went to bed full of expectation of a first-class climb on the morrow.

A downpour of rain and rumbles of thunder at midnight made us uneasy. If this continued, Trakta's slabs would rapidly become a hopeless proposition. Lofoten climbers may get caught in rain but they do not go out in rain. Nor do they go for hard climbs on wet rock. Rulten had shown us the wisdom of this. It did continue, and when we looked out at 7 a.m. there was nothing to see but low creeping mists.

It was not a wasted day, however. We were invited down to the house for " mid-dag ", and they did us proud, with the very fish that had looked like old wellington boots hanging on a line. This dried and salted cod is delicious, and it was cooked to perfection with a fine white sauce, and laced with crisp bacon and potatoes. After that we had jellied bilberries with sugar and cream.

While it lashed down outside, we were warm and snug inside, doing little else but eat and talk. To please the ladies I finished up by telling their fortunes from the tea-cups, and though they professed not to believe, it was amusing to see them hanging on to every word as if my inspiration was derived from some mystical source.

There was a weather transformation next day, as the ground fairly steamed with warmth and the hay rapidly dried. It was time we gave them our services for this important crop, and we had a busy morning, stacking the stuff on long frames till we had a few new rows of bright green. As in everything associated with farming, there is quite an art in stacking these frames. The scythed crop has to be shaken into neat bundles and folded over the wires. Even the shortest grass is cut and made into heaps —no easy job in country so steep that a false swing will blunt the scythe.

By afternoon the job was done, and we crossed by boat to the opposite island of Store Molla to climb a little thumb of rock that had intrigued us since coming here. It was only 1,500 feet, and birch trees wound up its slopes for half its height. The Raftsund peaks were in shadow while we were in sunshine, and the contrast of scene was amazing. On this side the colours were brilliant, from the green of ferns and silver birches, to the red granite of our rock thumb projecting against moving cloud. The other side was a study in black, ebony rocks shooting out of the sea to up-held finger points. A tiny dot of white on that dark shore showed that Lars was still in camp.

The thumb gave a pleasant scramble on its south side, and from the top we looked down on the community of Digermulen, the crofting metropolis of this part of the world. Eastwards the mainland peaks were hazy, trailing clouds that reached like glaciers to the sea. The glory of that evening resolved us on an early start in the morning for a climb on the biggest and sharpest peak of this island.

Whenever we went for a high peak in Lofoten we seemed to play our cards wrongly. If we started at midnight the weather always went bad on us, and we had the mortification of returning to camp as the sun heralded a clearing. If we climbed by day, we invariably returned to a night so warm and pleasant that it made a penance of trying to sleep. On the whole we nursed a grievance against the midnight sol.

This morning we thought Old Nick was in our favour. At 4 a.m. the sea was a calm blue and every boulder on the mountain tops was bathed in golden light. This should be the day of days for views, and from the adjacent island we should get a wonderful impression of the range on which we had spent so much time climbing. Moreover, the peak had a sharp rock *arête* which promised a good route to the top.

To our chagrin, the clouds were obscuring the sun and a wind had risen by the time we hauled out the boat. By 6 a.m. it was a grey morning. We rowed across the sound, catching a fish or two en route. A thick crop of birches and boulders screened us from the base of our peak. Our limbs moved with a distinct lassitude and we felt like consigning the peak to the Devil as we forced our way through. Staleness was creeping in.

Thankfully we got onto the rocks and at once we livened up. The ridge thinned almost immediately to a knife-edge. We climbed unroped, avoiding pinnacles by exposed traverses, and climbing sometimes on the north side, sometimes on the south, sometimes with a heel in both of these directions. Above a sharp-pointed top, we joined the main wall of the mountain and climbed by chimney and slab to the summit.

This is a rich island by comparison with its surroundings, with a westward strip of good land on the edge of peat and good hill grazing. Horses can be used as an aid in farming this gentle strip, and as a result, the hay crop was well gathered. The weather was dull and cold by now, with visibility so poor that it was hardly worth waiting on top for it to clear. We retired, and had the mortification of getting back to camp as the sun blazed through in full strength. To cheer up the party I made a great dumpling that had a visible effect on morale.

An even more enlivening event was the arrival of

Esther's girl friend Kirsty, a blonde, six feet tall with a command of English and a complexion that sent a sparkle to the lack-lustre eyes of Scott and Watson. Weir may not have been far behind. The disappointments of Store Molla were promptly forgotten in the good company of these fine girls. Far from being stale, I could detect an animation around me that showed there was still a fair whack of vitality in the party.

Unfortunately that night was our last in Lofoten.

The Road South

SOMETHING seemed to have happened to the weather. It had been fair for the best part of twenty-four hours, and it was still fine for our last morning. There was a total absence of wind, and though the time was only 6 a.m., the air was as balmy as a summer day in Kent.

No one in the house was stirring as we climbed for a last look at the green lake on the flank of Rulten. We had vague ideas of climbing a little pinnacle that projected from a narrow neck into the corrie. My ambitions were at a low ebb this warm day. From the flat of my back the mountains had an allure quickly dispelled by the sweat of getting there. As this feeling comes rarely to active mountaineers I felt like indulging it, particularly as ripe bilberry plants were everywhere at hand, hanging with luscious fruit.

Adam felt very much as I did, but not Scott. He had soon left us behind, and we lolled by the glacier pool watching the curve of waterfalls glisten in silvery spray, or listening to the pleasant drone of bees busy on the pink and yellow flowers around us.

Lower down on the hill we could see the whole family out searching the hillside. We soon joined them, and saw with interest that they were gathering bilberries at high speed with the aid of a little box fitted with a wire comb. Looping the comb through the clump of berries the wires pulled off the fruit, dropping them neatly into the little box. It was a clever arrangement and their pans were quickly filled.

Scott joined us at lunch-time as the sky became overcast and thundery. The family became galvanized into activity. Everything was dropped to get the cut hay to the barn before the rain came. The boys staggered under great trusses, making journey after journey to the barn. Everyone from grandmother to youngest child stripped the frames and loaded the crop into nets. There was even a small boat loaded high with it shuttling back and forth over the water.

We were too busy packing up to give them a hand. As work is taboo on a Sunday in Lofoten, this activity was quite unusual. Our concern was getting a lift to Svolvær to catch the 10 o'clock boat south to Bergen. With all this activity going on, we felt a bit guilty when everyone left the field to join us in coffee and to pay us their last respects.

The energetic Clara, who had teased the life out of us, rushed to get her carpet, unrolling it proudly to exhibit my second pair of trousers, now a distinguished strip of jungle green in a magnificently coloured stair-carpet. We had never met anyone quite like Clara. Whether walking in the fields, spinning or hay making, she had a vitality in her movements and a sparkle in her eye that was a joy to see. Right now she pretended to be in tears as she saw us off.

A boat had been sighted, and the two stalwarts, Esther and Kirsty, rowed us out to intercept it. Lifts are the custom in Lofoten. No boat will ever refuse, and our luck was right in here, for we crashed into a " party ". Willing hands pulled our stuff on board, and with cheery waves the girls departed.

At once we were plied with coffee, and the contents of the galley were spread out for everyone to tuck in. They were a merry crowd from Kabelvaäg, a village which is connected by the road south from Svolvær. They were on their way home after a picnic in the Trollfjord. Two tall brothers with an excellent command of English took us in hand.

We told them of our doings in the last few weeks and they were horrified to hear that we had not stayed in Kabelvaag. Kabelvaag was the true cultural heart of Lofoten with a church that went back to 1100. No one can know Lofoten until they have stayed in Kabelvaag. We were urged to go home with them there and then.

Certainly they were good advocates of this paragon of places, and they looked forward to the time when their studies in Oslo would be completed and they could come back and live permanently in the north. With them was a most beautiful little girl with the brightest eyes we had ever seen. Her alert expression and fine features would have commanded attention anywhere. She was a classical dancer who had danced ballet in Paris and London, and her eyes lit with pleasure when she saw we were interested in the dance and could talk of it. We shall look out for her name on the Glasgow bills.

Svolvæer came all too soon. The mail boat was already tugging at its moorings as we threw our stuff aboard. Adam was not with us. He elected to stay north for another week, and try his luck with a trawler from Lodingen or Tromso. He got it too, thereby saving a fare of £15.

Among the smartly dressed people thronging the quay his battered anorak and much stained army trousers were conspicuous. The lot was topped by a dense crop of red hair and the beginnings of a ginger beard. He had a hankering to see the southern island of Moskenesöy and intended to go there after a night in Svolvæer. We missed his cheery company, but it appears that we missed more by not going to Moskenesöy, for the cliff scenery is quite incredible.

Beyond our bow, standing out of the grey sea like an iron wedge, was the rock peak of Vaagekallentind that had beaten us so near its pointed top. Against an oppressive mass of rain clouds the razor edges of the Raftsund were the mountains of our dreams, inaccessible and uncompromising, showing their teeth even from here. The rain had held off and the hay would now be safely gathered in the barn below them.

It was cold, and we were glad to spread our sleeping-bags and crawl under a lifeboat, trying to shut out the wheezing of an incessant accordion and the droning songs of drunken men. There was no dearth of accordion players—as one went off another came on. The tunes were the same monotonous jazz ditties. We were partly successful until a drunk thought he had discovered a soft seat.

Rain marred what could have been a wonderful sail to Bergen. The high mountains were buried in clouds, and for mile after mile we might have been steaming past the same belt of coast, with houses perched like boxes on the most inhospitable and unlikely places. Only when you have steamed like this for three and a half days do you realize that a population of 3,000,000 is a devil of a big number when you see a fraction of it strung out in this way. Yet it is less than half the population of Greater London.

The passengers were interesting. There were young Norwegians who had been cycling in Finnmark, sixteen years old, six feet tall, and full of the joys of life ; a young Swiss waiter who had been to the North Cape and who was willing to discourse in English, French, German, Italian, or Norwegian ; a knowledgeable fisherman who told us that 80 million hectolitres of herrings had been taken on this coast last year ; and a young English couple who spoke to nobody, but went around wrapped in oilskins, Baedeker and map in hand, gazing earnestly at heaven knows what. All we could see were misty headlands, though it was a pleasant surprise to find kittiwake gulls nesting on window ledges above the picturesque harbour of Ålasund.

Rather typically, we were prodded to wakefulness in Bergen. Most of the passengers were already off the ship while we lay blissfully asleep below our groundsheet. It was still raining as we packed up.

In case the Norsk Tourist Bureau should sue me for libelling their weather, I should explain that this was not only a bad summer, but one of the worst in living memory. Nor was it confined to Norway. All Europe had it, and in Glasgow, when I arrived, the rain was even heavier than any I had seen in Norway. The latter statement is not advanced as proof.

Lofoten Birds

WITH three ornithologists in the party a word or two should perhaps be said on the birds of these islands. The admission must be made straightaway that little serious watching was attempted. When the weather was good we were climbing, when it was bad we were sleeping, so my remarks are more or less confined to what we saw in passing.

The paucity of ducks and waders was one of the major surprises of these islands. In fact we saw only three species of the latter, oyster-catcher, redshank, and sandpipers, and these were distributed thinly, much more thinly than on the west coast of Scotland. On the other hand, eider ducks were much more numerous than we are accustomed to see in Scotland, and red-breasted mergansers were common. No other ducks were seen.

The hawk tribe was represented by eagles, both golden and white-tailed. The white-tailed was viewed from above as it swung in slow circles, its conspicuous patch of white being quite unmistakable. The long wings were magnificently controlled as it banked to each updraught of air, the great primaries like outstretched hands reminding us of the broad-winged Griffon vultures of the Himalayas.

The white-tailed eagle is a remorseless hunter, all being fish that comes to its net. It will eat anything, from hens to lambs, so it is little wonder that it is extinct as a breeding species in Britain. We saw this bird only once, on the flank of Rulten as we climbed, and as we did not see it again during our stay at Reknes, it seems unlikely that it was breeding in the vicinity, though the terrain was ideally suited, with trees, marshes, and cliffs—all favourite sites. The last breeding of the species in Scotland was in 1916, in Skye, so it looks as if we in Britain have lost this powerful bird for ever.

I have mentioned the prevalence of the magpie in Lofoten, and indeed the bird is met with in strength all over Norway. It is a popular bird, but not quite so common as the hooded crow, which is everywhere. Another popular bird is the starling. Nesting boxes are provided to encourage them, as they are said to have a cheering influence about the place with their " nutcracking " and whistling. They were not over-common. Ravens were well distributed.

Most interesting to us were the large numbers of willow grouse frequenting the woods. As mentioned earlier in the text, these white-winged birds sound much like our own grouse in their harsh " go-back, go-back ", and not until they open their wings is there very much difference in plumage. We were surprised to hear that they provide the main diet for the large numbers of foxes infesting Lofoten. Higher up on the mountains we came across that other member of the grouse family, the ptarmigan, which also turns white in winter. These were by no means as common as in Scotland. Snow-buntings were other sparse nesters on the high tops.

The fringes of the shore, where the burns emptied through birch woods and hayfields, were the places richest in bird life. Here one might find something of everything, the singing of wrens amongst the boulders, flocks of twites foraging the hayfields ; among the birches might be fieldfares, redwings, mealy redpolls, bramblings and house sparrows ; by the burn, dipper and white wagtail ; perhaps ring-ouzels rising in alarm from bilberry clumps, white collar flashing on dark mantle.

We saw only one member of the titmouse family, and that was on the crags of Rulten, and it was so difficult to see that we were unable to identify its species.

The commonest birds were undoubtedly wheatears, meadow pipits, and tree pipits. We saw no rock pipits, though the country was ideally suited for them.

On the sea there was little of outstanding interest. Of the gulls there were the common, herring, lesser black-backed, and greater black-backed. Of skuas, only the Arctic skua in its dark phase was seen. Arctic terns and black guillemots were common.

For land and sea we recorded only thirty-five positive species. This, of course, does include varieties seen on the tundra of Hjerkinn or at Lyngen.

Anyone going to watch birds should pay more attention to the more marshy and low-lying islands such as Gimsoy. There are also fine cliffs on Moskenesöy where the auks congregate in large numbers. A visit there would be rich in reward.

LOFOTEN
AND THE
RAFTSUND

HINNÖY

Raftsund

BLAAFJELL

Trollfjord

Trollfjordvand
STORE
TROLLTIND

HIGRAFSTIND

BRAKSET

Camp Konsnes
Kofhopvatn

RORHOPTIND

RULTEN

REKNES

SLOTHMOLLEN

DIGERMULEN

STORE MOLLA

Öyhellsund

"GOAT"

SVOLVÆR

Kabelvaag

LITTLE MOLLA

AUSTVAAGÖY

GIMSÖY

Camp

VAAGEKALLEN

Hadsel Fjord

Vest Fjord

N

MILES   0   5   10   15   20   25

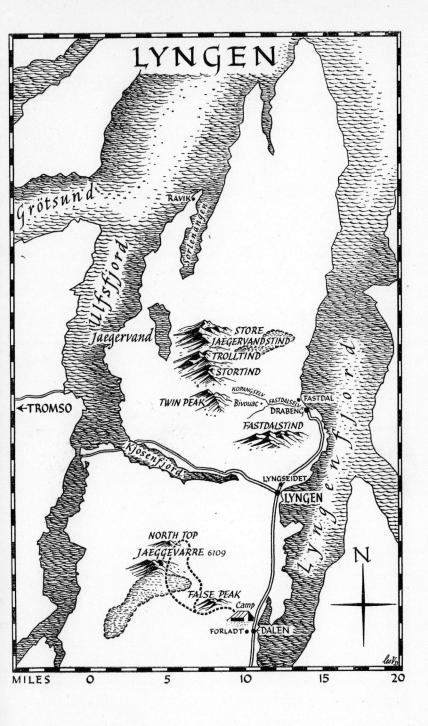

LYNGEN

Grötsund

Ravik.

Ulfsfjord

Orienangen

Jaegervand

STORE
JAEGERVANDSTIND

TROLLTIND

STORTIND

←TROMSO

TWIN PEAK   KOPANGSELV
              Bivouac   FASTDALSELV   FASTDAL
                         DRABENG
              FASTDALSTIND

Kjosenfjord

Lyngen fjord

LYNGSEIDET

LYNGEN

NORTH TOP
JAEGGEVARRE 6109

N

FALSE PEAK   Camp
               DALEN
FORLADT•

leoV.

MILES   O   5   10   15   20